same same but different

by POH

ABC Books

To my little blowfly with no wings. Zed, Tara, Jordan & Sunny Day

Dear Cooks,

The idea for this book came to me from years of cooking and sharing recipes. I often come away surprised and comforted by how much we are linked through the language of flavour even when there seems to be a gulf of differences between cultures. Whether it be the way an ingredient is used or textures we gravitate to, we are still fundamentally drawn to making things a certain way because the instinct is universal. On one of my trips to Southeast Asia the phrase 'Same Same But Different' struck me as the perfect four words to tie my idea together.

I'm no chef and I'm proud of it. For me the joy in what I do is all about representing home cooks. I always want to write books that honestly reflect how I cook every day, which is how every Aussie cooks – one day I'm making puff pastry from scratch and the next I'm tucking into a bowl of 2-minute noodles! More than anything I want you to USE this book. I hope I inspire you to make a mess in your kitchen and get these pages dirty.

Giggles and guffaws,

Poh x

p.s. Please read 'A Few Things to Get You Over the Line' on the next page.

A Few Things to Get You Over the Line

Timing

For very quick cooking or sautéing, you will notice I avoid times and instead give visual cues. This is because relying on timing when it's mere seconds is a risky business. I wish more recipes were written like this these days – if we want to aspire to be good cooks, we need to engage with a recipe using our senses more than our watches and timers. There are so many variables – quality of heat, using a different-sized pan, accuracy of temperature, halving the ingredients – all these things will affect the outcome, so using your instinct is your most accurate guide.

Sourcing Ingredients

Please don't wig out at the mention of an exotic ingredient! I've given you photos at the back of the book of every uncommon ingredient I've used so you can recognise things like packaging and alternative names and shop with more confidence. I haven't gone into comprehensive detail with regard to history and descriptions of each ingredient because it's 2014 and we have the internet. My main aim is to help you spot these ingredients on the shelves of Asian grocers or supermarkets if you've never encountered them before.

Making Pastry by Machine

In most of the pastry methods I avoid a food processor. This is just a personal preference because for me, the good old-fashioned way seems to yield better results. However, I suspect it might be that I possess the ideal 'cold hands' for the job. If you have cursed hot hands, pulse the prescribed amount of butter with all the dry ingredients in a food processor until you have a sandy texture, then add small amounts of chilled water, pulsing until the mixture pulls into a single mass. The rest is the same as the handmade method.

Making Rempahs by Machine

For processing all the Malaysian rempahs (wet aromatic pastes) in the book, I always recommend using a good-quality blender or a small food processor. The smaller cavity of small food processors will create a whirlpool and chop ingredients very finely or even purée, but a large food processor will only chop finely and this is still not fine enough for very woody or fibrous ingredients like galangal and lemongrass. A blender will liquefy or purée with the help of liquid and the difference between a good and bad blender is the smell of a burnt engine, especially when you are dealing with strong vegetable fibres!

or by hand

If you don't mind a bit of hard yakka, using a mortar and pestle is another option but very time consuming. All old Malaysian 'aunties' insist it tastes better using the old-fashioned method but I must confess that the convenience of electricity is all too seductive! If you want to have an authentic experience, lay down a square metre of old newspaper and pound while squatting. Add small amounts at a time, pounding from the most robust textured ingredients to the softer ones, only adding more when you have made a fine paste from the previous batch. Scoop the contents out from time to time to accommodate more aromatics.

Vegetarians

I'm aware not all my 'vegetarian' dishes are properly vego because of the use of fish-based seasonings but I trust you can look after yourselves. For oyster sauce substitute with mushroom oyster sauce, for fish sauce substitute with light soy or tamari.

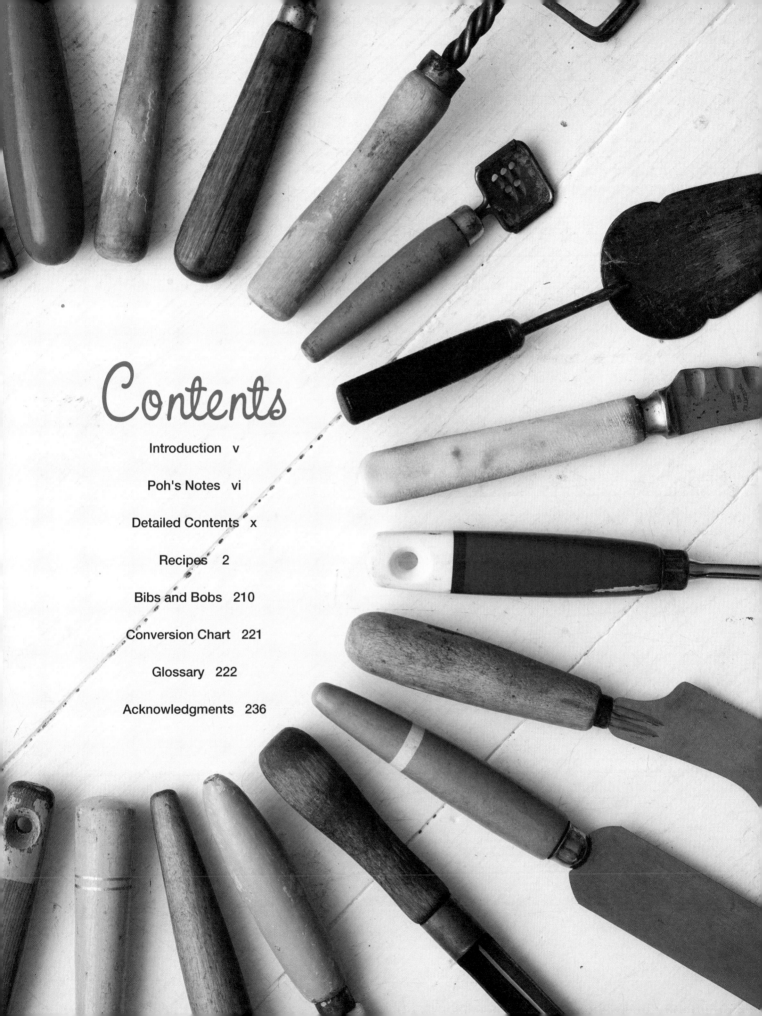

Contents

Tarts & Pies

Classics

Chocolate

Spreads

Bibs & Bobs

From Scratch

Basics

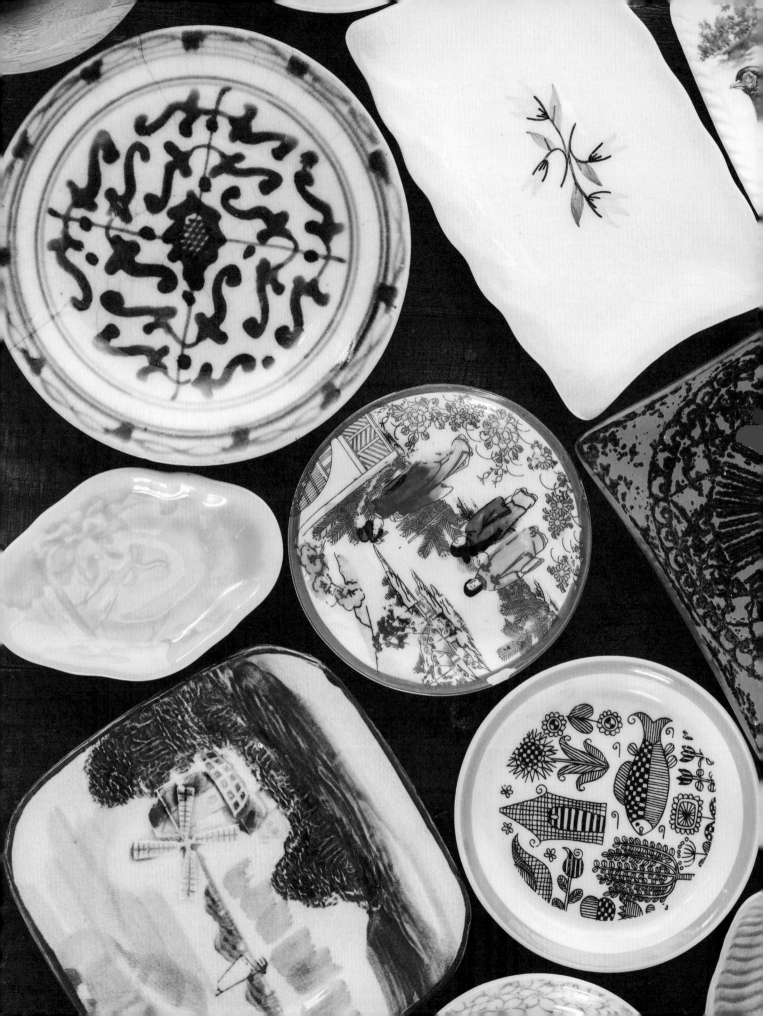

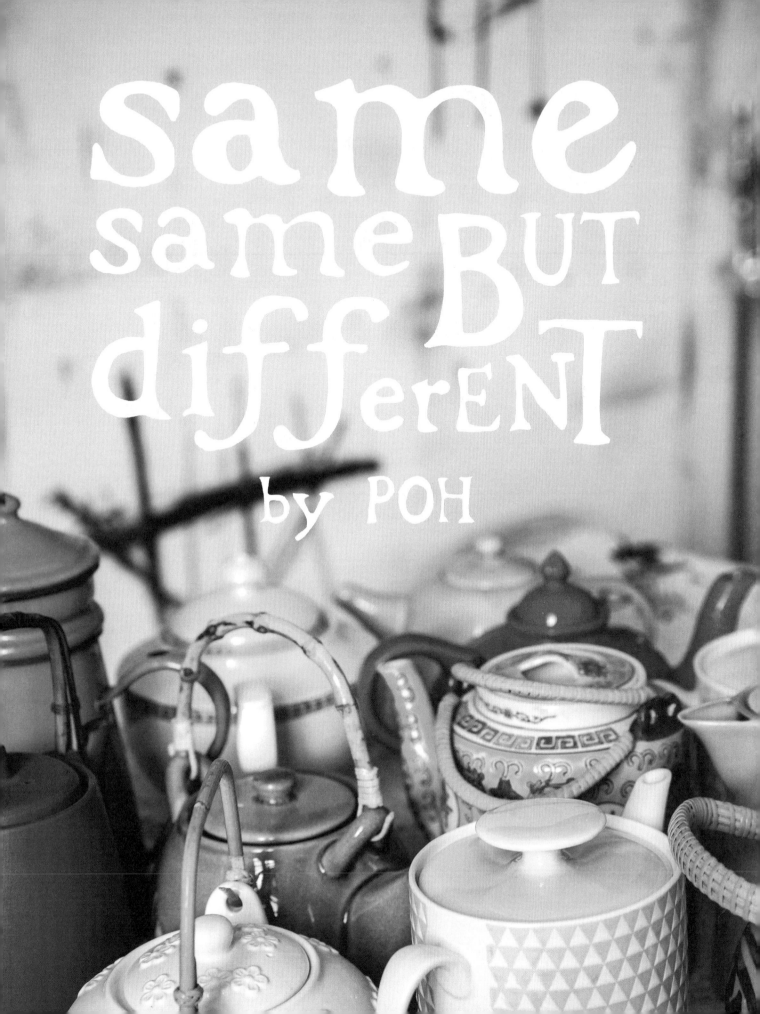

same same but different

by POH

Bite-Sized Spice

Kunyit (Turmeric) Fried Chicken

This Malaysian favourite is ridiculously simple to put together. It's excellent as a casual starter or finger food and makes a superb beer snack. I must warn you to smack away any greedy fingers lurking around when you cook it up or you might find your portions somewhat dwindled!

2kg chicken wings, wingtip and
    drumette separated, OR legs

3 cloves garlic, peeled and finely
    chopped

2 teaspoons light soy sauce

2 tablespoons ground turmeric

2 teaspoons ground coriander

1 teaspoon ground ginger

1–2 teaspoons chilli powder, OR to taste

2 teaspoons salt, crushed into very fine
    grains with a mortar and pestle

10 sprigs of fresh curry leaves

1½ L vegetable, peanut OR ricebran oil

Special Equipment: disposable gloves + large snaplock bag

Combine the chicken pieces, garlic and soy in a bowl and toss to coat evenly. Mix the turmeric, coriander, ginger, chilli and salt in a small bowl and pour over the chicken. Wearing disposable gloves (because turmeric stains with a vengeance) mix with your hands until the chicken is thoroughly covered with the spices and seasoning. Scrunch the curry leaves roughly in your hands and nestle them amongst the chicken pieces then transfer into a snaplock bag pushing as much air out of the bag as possible before sealing OR place in a bowl and cover with cling wrap. Marinate in the fridge over 1–2 nights for a superior result OR a minimum of 2 hours.

Heat the oil in a medium saucepan or wok over medium–high heat. To test the oil, rest the tips of your chopsticks on the bottom of the saucepan and if a flurry of bubbles rises rapidly to the surface, you are good to go. Always do a test-fry with a single piece of chicken. If the oil is too hot the chicken will burn on the outside before it is cooked all the way through.

Fry 5–6 pieces of chicken at a time, for about 5–7 minutes per batch, together with the curry leaves (beware, these will spit violently) as this will make the oil beautifully fragrant. The result should be a deep golden brown with a vibrant yellow tint and the outside of the chicken wonderfully crunchy. Rest the cooked chicken on kitchen towel in a colander. Repeat until all chicken is cooked.

Serve with the fried curry leaves (which are to be eaten).

If using chicken legs score twice across the fattest part of the flesh all the way to the bone. This will help the chicken cook through easier. Also, factor in a longer cooking time.

Curry Puffs

Learning how to crimp a curry puff perfectly is one of my earliest food memories. From the age of six, I used to practise obsessively on playdough. If you can't manage the crimping, the job is easily done by using the tips of a fork to press down on the seams. As long as they're adequately sealed they will go down the same way. For those longing for a sauce, there is no need – these moreish little parcels are a crowd pleaser packed full of flavour and are traditionally eaten as is.

Filling

2 tablespoons vegetable oil

½ large brown onion, peeled, diced into 5mm cubes

2–3 tablespoons meat curry powder*

250g chicken breast OR chuck steak, diced into 5mm cubes OR use mince if you are too lazy

100g sweet potato, peeled, diced into 5mm cubes

1 medium potato, peeled, diced into 5mm cubes

½ teaspoon sugar, OR to taste

1 teaspoon salt, OR to taste

Shortcrust Pastry

3⅓ cups (500g) plain flour

1 teaspoon salt

250g unsalted butter, room temperature

120ml chilled water + more if required

OR

1kg store-bought shortcrust pastry

2 L vegetable oil, for frying

To make the *filling*, heat the oil in a medium sized non-stick frypan over medium heat and sauté the onions for about 2 minutes OR until soft and golden. Add the meat curry powder and cook for about 10 seconds OR until toasted and very fragrant. Add the chicken and stir-fry until cooked. Add the remaining ingredients and stir-fry for about 5 minutes OR until the potatoes are tender. Taste and season further. Spread mixture out on a plate to cool, cover with cling wrap and refrigerate.

To make the *shortcrust pastry*, combine the flour, salt and butter in a large mixing bowl. Break off chunks of butter and, with your hands, rub the butter into the flour vigorously until you achieve a sandy consistency. Gradually add tablespoons of water and, rather than kneading, use a gathering, squeezing action to bind the mixture into a firm dough. Roughly shape into 3 discs, cover with cling wrap and rest in the fridge for 30 minutes.

To stuff curry puffs, dust a clean benchtop with a little flour and roll pastry until 3mm thick. Cut 20 circles with a pastry cutter – cut all your pastry out at once then lay the cut pieces on baking paper, cover with cling wrap and place in fridge. Working with only a few pieces out of the fridge at a time, fill each circle with a teaspoonful of mixture, fold in half then squeeze the edges together and crimp OR using the tips of a fork, gently press on the seams (resting on benchtop) to seal the edges. Place the curry puffs on a tray in the fridge until ready to cook.

To fry, heat the oil over medium–high heat in a large saucepan OR wok. To test if the oil is ready, drop in a very small portion of pastry. If it turns golden in 15–20 seconds, you are good to go. Fry 4 curry puffs at a time until the pastry is a beautiful deep golden, then drain in a colander lined with paper towel. Another option is to brush the curry puffs with an egg wash (1 egg whisked with 1 tablespoon milk) and bake at 180°C or 170°C fan-forced for about 25–30 minutes until deep golden. Serve hot or at room temperature.

Don't waste pastry scraps! Leave at room temperature and knead scraps into a ball, then flatten into a disc, cover in cling wrap and freeze for a rainy day. Don't try to use the scraps right away (the gluten needs to relax overnight) or you will have a hard time rolling it out and it will shrink dramatically when cooked. If you are saving store-bought pastry, trim the dry edges off before kneading into a ball. Make sure you weigh and date the dough before freezing.

*Available from Asian grocers

Sour Power

Kimchi

If there was ever a dish that I would describe as a culinary 'punch in the face', this is definitely it! This humble pickle is so loved in Korea, it is considered THE national dish and hundreds of its kind exist. When my sister-in-law, Teena, gave me this recipe I was quite surprised at the number of ingredients and the detailed process, but I guess there had to be a reason behind the riot of flavour that defines this wonderfully moreish pickle. I once watched a Korean lady eating it with cake – this is how much Koreans adore kimchi!

1¼ large fresh wombok* (Chinese cabbage), outer leaves discarded, quartered lengthways, stem left intact

1 cup cooking salt (not all of this has to be used)

1 heaped tablespoon glutinous rice flour*

½ cup (125ml) water

5 cloves garlic, peeled and roughly sliced

3cm piece of ginger, peeled, finely sliced

¼ nashi pear OR green apple, peeled, cored, sliced

¼ medium brown onion, peeled, sliced

200g Chinese radish*, peeled and sliced

⅔ cup aka gochugaru (Korean chilli powder)*

½ cup (125ml) fish sauce

2 tablespoons caster sugar

6 spring onions, sliced 4cm long on a steep diagonal

Special Equipment: food processor OR blender + disposable gloves

Plunge the cabbage quarters into a large bowl of water and spread the leaves apart to make sure the water reaches the base of each leaf. Drain cabbage quarters briefly in a colander. Pry leaves apart and sprinkle each layer with a light coating of salt – the base of the leaves can be salted more generously. Allow the salted cabbage to rest in a bowl for 2 hours OR until cabbage stalks are wilted but still make a crisp sound when snapped. Rinse leaves well under running water, drain for 20–30 minutes, then squeeze out the excess moisture.

To make the pickling sauce, combine the glutinous rice flour and water in a small saucepan, then cook over medium heat, stirring continuously, for about 1 minute OR until the mixture turns into a thick, milky paste. Set aside to cool.

Combine the garlic, ginger, nashi, onion and Chinese radish in a food processor OR blender and blitz into a pulpy paste. Transfer to a medium mixing bowl and mix thoroughly with the cooled glutinous rice paste, chilli powder, fish sauce, sugar and spring onions. Wearing disposable gloves, lay cabbage quarters on a baking tray and thoroughly coat each layer of cabbage leaves with the paste. Cut stalks away then, holding the quarters in place, slice 3cm segments across cabbage. Transfer and gently press cabbage into an airtight container (glass bottomed is best), pour remaining pickling sauce over the top and seal. Leave in a cool dark place to ferment. Taste after 3 days to check the acidity level is to your liking and that the cabbage is tender but with a residual crunch. If not, ferment for another day or two and taste again. Transfer container to the fridge and keep for up to 3 months.

Serve kimchi cold as part of a shared meal, as a snack with rice and fried Korean seaweed (my favourite) or add to noodle soups and hot roast meat sandwiches – it goes especially well with pork.

*Available from Asian grocers

Basic Chinese Pickles

These pickles are excellent in sandwiches with things like roast meats (especially pork), in salads, on cold rolls and are a lively, cleansing accompaniment to have with fried food.

Pickling Liquid

2 cups (500ml) white vinegar OR half rice vinegar will give a more complex flavour

2 cups (440g) white sugar

Vegetables

350g cabbage, sliced into 1.5cm strips

2 medium carrots, peeled, halved lengthways and sliced diagonally into 2–3mm thick pieces

½ continental cucumber, quartered lengthways, seeds sliced off and discarded, sliced diagonally into 2–3mm thick pieces

1 teaspoon salt

To make the *pickling liquid*, combine the vinegars and sugar in a small saucepan and cook over medium heat, stirring until sugar is dissolved. Set aside to cool completely.

Combine all the *vegetables* in a colander, sprinkle with the salt and toss well. Leave the vegetables to wilt in the fridge for 1–2 hours. Transfer the colander to the sink and, using the palm of your hand, gently push on the mound of vegetables to remove any excess moisture. Spoon the vegetables into a large sterilised glass jar and pour pickling liquid over the top. Don't be concerned if the liquid doesn't quite cover the vegetables for the time being as more liquid will wilt out of the vegetables overnight.

These pickles are best eaten within a week and will keep well for up to 2 weeks in the refrigerator, but after this they will become less vibrant in flavour and colour.

Pork & Purses

Chinese Pork & Cabbage Dumplings

Feeds 2 for a main meal, 4 for a starter

Dumplings are the definitive Chinese peasant food but no matter where your cultural heritage lies, there's no denying these little parcels are the ultimate comfort food. The sensation of chomping into one of these plump parcels and its juices squirting down your chin is unbeatable. And before you start thinking it's all too hard, remember many hands make light work – this is a great recipe for a communal effort.

Dumpling Skins

1 cup (150g) plain flour
110ml freshly boiled water

Spicy Dipping Sauce

¼ cup (60ml) light soy sauce
2 tablespoons Chinkiang vinegar*
⅛ teaspoon sugar
2–3 teaspoons Chinese chilli oil*
1 tablespoon finely shredded ginger
2 teaspoons finely chopped garlic

Filling

½ teaspoon salt
200g Chinese cabbage* (wombok)
    finely shredded
280g pork mince
1 tablespoon finely chopped ginger
⅓ cup spring onions OR Chinese
    chives, chopped
⅛ teaspoon ground white pepper
¼ cup (60ml) chicken stock OR water
1½ tablespoons light soy sauce
1 tablespoon shaoxing rice wine*
1 tablespoon vegetable oil
1 tablespoon sesame oil

Special Equipment: dumpling roller (from Asian grocer) OR a 2cm x 20cm piece of dowel

To make the *dumpling skins*, place the flour in a medium mixing bowl, make a well at the centre and pour in the boiling water. Using chopsticks or a fork, stir until you get a crumbly mixture. Once the dough is cool enough to handle, tip the mixture onto a clean benchtop and knead for about 5 minutes OR until you have a smooth, firm-ish ball of dough, adding more water or flour along the way if necessary. Cover with cling wrap and rest for 10 minutes.

To make the *spicy dipping sauce*, mix all the ingredients together and set aside.

To make the *filling*, mix the salt with the cabbage and allow to sit for 15 minutes to draw out the excess water. Rinse the cabbage before squeezing well to remove as much liquid as possible. In a medium mixing bowl, combine cabbage with the remaining filling ingredients and mix until combined.

To make the dumplings, sprinkle the dough with some plain flour and roll into 2–3 cylinders, 3cm in diameter. Cut into 2cm thick discs and flatten with the palm of your hand then cover them with an overturned bowl to keep them moist.

With a dumpling rolling pin, roll inwards only (to maintain an even circle) from the outer edge of each disc to the centre. Roll the skins until they are 1mm thick. Stuff a teaspoonful of the filling into the centre of each wrapper, fold and seal. When crimping pleat only one side of the dumpling – this will pull the dumpling into a traditional crescent shape. If this sounds too difficult, pinching to seal the seam well is the basic goal.

To cook the dumplings, bring a large pot of salted water to the boil. Lower as many dumplings as you wish into the water and wait for them to float. Cook for a further 10 seconds before scooping the dumplings out with a slotted spoon and transferring them to a well-oiled tray or plate. For a crispy finish, pan-fry the boiled dumplings with some oil in a large non-stick frypan over medium heat until the bottoms are golden brown. Serve immediately, crispy bottoms facing upwards, with the spicy dipping sauce.

*Available from Asian grocers

Crystal Skin Yam Bean Purses

Most people will find the textures and flavours in this recipe unfamiliar territory in a dumpling. Between a slightly chewy translucent skin, the crunch and sweetness of yam bean, and the robust pungency of shiitake mushrooms and dried shrimp is an intriguing dumpling experience.

Filling

½ cup shiitake mushrooms*

⅔ cup dried shrimp*

2–3 tablespoons vegetable oil

2 cloves garlic, peeled, finely chopped

3 cups (285g) yam bean*, peeled and cut into 2cm long matchsticks or coarsely grated

1 large carrot, peeled, coarsely grated

4–5 spring onions, chopped

1 cup lightly packed chopped coriander, including stalks

3 teaspoons oyster sauce

¼–½ teaspoon fish sauce

½ teaspoon caster sugar

⅛ teaspoon ground white pepper

Garlic Oil

¼ cup (60ml) vegetable oil

1 clove garlic, peeled, chopped

Crystal Dumpling Skins

215g wheat starch OR wheaten cornflour

20g potato starch*

90g tapioca starch/flour*

350ml boiling water

Chinese chilli oil OR Asian-style garlic chilli sauce for dipping*

*Available from Asian grocers

Special Equipment: dumpling roller (from Asian grocer) OR a 2cm x 20cm piece of dowel + large bamboo steamer

To make the *filling*, place the dried shiitake in a bowl and cover with freshly boiled water for 20 minutes OR until completely softened. Drain and finely slice. Soak the dried shrimp in hot water for 20 minutes, then squeeze to remove excess moisture and finely chop.

Heat the oil and garlic in a large non-stick frypan OR wok over high heat until the garlic develops some colour around the edges. Add the shrimp and shiitake and stir-fry until the shrimp begins to turn golden and pop. Add the yam bean and carrot and stir-fry for another minute, then add the spring onions, coriander, oyster sauce, fish sauce, sugar and white pepper. Mix and taste, then balance with more fish sauce and sugar if required. Set aside to cool.

To make the *garlic oil* for basting, combine the oil and garlic in a small saucepan over medium heat and cook until the garlic is golden. Remove from the heat as soon as the garlic begins to colour or the residual heat might burn it. Set aside to cool.

To make the *dumpling skins*, combine the starches in a large bowl. Add 350ml of freshly boiled water and stir with a fork or chopsticks to form a dough. Once the dough is cool enough to handle, tip the mixture onto a clean benchtop and knead until smooth and pliable. Roll the dough into a fat cylinder, 3–4cm in diameter. Cut the cylinder in half and cover with cling wrap.

Slice each cylinder into 8–10 equal pieces. Squash each disc flat with the palm of your hand, then keep them covered in cling wrap while working with one disc at a time. Using a dumpling rolling pin, roll inwards only from the outer edge of each disc to the centre to maintain an even circle. If the dough is sticking to the benchtop, dust a tiny amount of wheat starch over the bench and if sticking to your hands rub some vegetable oil onto them. Roll skins until 2mm thick and stuff with a dessertspoon full of yam bean mixture, then fold in half and pinch to seal well. Crimp with a pretty edge if you are able or leave as is. This dough is quite pliable so even if you overstuff it slightly it's not likely to burst.

To steam the purses, line a large bamboo steamer with baking paper pierced with a few holes and brush generously with the garlic oil. Arrange the dumplings with a 1–2cm space between each one. Brush the tops of the dumplings with the garlic oil and steam over high heat for 10–15 minutes. Traditionally these dumplings are eaten plain or served with Chinese chilli oil or an Asian-style garlic chilli sauce.

Boil, Bake, Steam

Bagels

The first time I ever had bagels was in America. I was fourteen and enamoured with the USA from watching too many '80s sitcoms. I dreamt of being picked up in highschool hallways by cute guys while getting books out of my locker and when I got there it wasn't far from my flaky teenage fantasies. My grandfather's good friends Arnie and Blessing Semler picked us up from LAX in a Cadillac and whisked us off to their son Ron's ranch, where the long-running hit soap *Dallas* was filmed. That afternoon bagels and other 'refreshments' were wheeled out on a trolley by the housekeeper onto a beautiful lawn. As we ate and watched the horses I developed an instant crush on the Semlers' grandson, Devin. Even now my favourite way to have bagels is with pastrami and Swiss cheese because that is how I had them that day.

7g dry yeast

2 tablespoons caster sugar

⅔ cup (160ml) warm milk

3 cups (450g) plain bread flour*, sifted

1 cup (150g) wholemeal bread flour*, sifted

1 teaspoon salt

⅔ cup (160ml) warm water + extra if needed

1 egg, lightly beaten

1 tablespoon poppy or sesame seeds (or any seed of your choice)

*I have made these many times with multi-purpose flour but bread flour is ideal.

Mix the yeast, sugar and milk in a small bowl. Cover and set aside for 10 minutes OR until the surface of the mixture is covered in bubbles.

Combine the flours and salt in a medium mixing bowl, make a well at the centre and add the yeast mixture and warm water. With clean hands, gather the dry ingredients into the centre until most of it is incorporated into one lumpy mass. Tip the mixture onto a clean benchtop and knead for about 5 minutes, adding a little extra water or flour if needed, until you have a smooth, pliable dough that is not sticking to the benchtop.

Roll the dough into a fat sausage, slice into 10 equal pieces and cover with a damp tea towel while you work with one piece at a time. Roll each piece into a sausage, 2cm in diameter. Dust the palm of your hand with a little flour and squash 2cm of one end of each sausage. Form a doughnut shape overlapping the tail end onto the flattened end, then pull the flattened part from both sides of the tail so they meet on top and pinch into a seam. Flip the bagel over and admire your work then place on baking trays lined with baking paper and cover with a slightly damp tea towel. Rest in a warm, draught-free spot for 15–45 minutes, depending on the temperature, until the bagels have doubled their original size.

Preheat the oven to 190°C or 180°C fan-forced. Bring a large saucepan of water to the boil and boil the bagels, in batches of 3 or 4, for 1 minute on each side. Remove with a slotted spoon and rest on a clean tea towel. They will look slightly deflated and dimply but don't be alarmed. Return the bagels to the baking trays lined with paper, brush generously with the beaten egg, then dip the top half into the seeds OR sprinkle them on. Bake for about 20 minutes OR until golden brown.

Serving suggestions
- Classic: fresh or toasted with a slather of cream cheese
- My favourite: pastrami and Swiss cheese
- Cream cheese, smoked salmon, some slices of polski ogorki (dill pickles), capers and a sprinkle of finely chopped chives

Chinese Steamed Flower Buns (Mantou)

Makes about 15 buns

As a child this was one of my favourite 'going out' foods. I have lovely memories of unravelling every sweet, marshmallowy thread and eating them individually. My first go at making these ended in tears and there's nothing I hate more than having a restless night feeling defeated by a recipe. Second time around I went to bed high on Flower Bun success and still didn't sleep a wink. Serve with any dish that has a lovely sauce to mop up or use in place of brioche buns for sliders.

Yeast Mixture

1 teaspoon dry yeast
20g caster sugar
100ml warm water

Dough

350g (2⅓ cups) plain flour
1 teaspoon baking powder, sifted
30g caster sugar
½ teaspoon salt
1 tablespoon melted vegetable shortening OR vegetable oil (but not olive)
100ml warm water + extra if needed
vegetable oil for basting

For more flavour, substitute the vegetable oil for basting with sesame oil and sprinkle chopped spring onions and toasted sesame seeds onto the cut threads before knotting into a flower. It is also an option to deep fry these after steaming if you want a crispy finish, but you will be saying hello to a few more calories!

Special Equipment: electric cake mixer with dough hook OR by hand + pasta maker OR rolling pin + pastry brush + large bamboo steamer (25cm diameter) with lid + a pot that the steamer will sit snuggly on

To make the *yeast mixture* combine the yeast and sugar in a small bowl, adding a tiny amount of the warm water to emulsify into a rough paste before mixing with the remaining warm water. Cover with cling wrap and set aside for 10 minutes OR until the surface of the mixture is covered in bubbles.

To make the *dough*, combine the flour, baking powder, sugar and salt in a large mixing bowl. Whisk briefly to mix the dry ingredients and make a well at the centre. If you are mixing by hand add the yeast mixture, vegetable shortening or oil and most but not all of the 100ml warm water to the well and gather the dry ingredients into the centre until mostly incorporated into a lumpy mass. Knead for about 5 minutes, adding a little extra water or flour if required, until you have a smooth, pliable dough that is not sticking to the benchtop. If using an electric cake mixer, tip all the ingredients, withholding a small amount of the water, into the mixing bowl and mix with a dough hook on 1st speed for about 3 minutes OR until smooth.

Transfer the dough into a large oiled bowl (glass is best) and cover with cling wrap. Allow to prove or rise in a warm, draught-free spot for 2–3 hours OR until double its original size. Punch the dough down and tear off a golfball-sized chunk (50–60g). Shape into a fat sausage, dust with a little flour and crank through a pasta maker on its 1st setting, then 2nd setting. Pass your flattened piece of dough through the fettuccine setting. As the noodles come out the other end, support the strands and guide them carefully onto the benchtop as a single sheet without scattering the noodles too much. Using a pastry brush, brush a good amount of oil over every thread. Hold the cluster of noodles at one end then wind the remaining length around your hand into a coil that resembles a hair bun, tucking the loose ends neatly underneath. Rest the bun on a small square of baking paper.

Repeat until all dough is used. Allow the buns to prove for 30–40 minutes OR until doubled in size (but no more – over-proving will create a slightly collapsed wrinkly result after steaming).

Place buns in a bamboo steamer over a saucepan half-filled with water, cover with lid and steam for 5–6 minutes over high heat then serve immediately. These store very well in an airtight container in a cool place for up to 10 days, so you can make them ahead of time for dinner parties and revive with a 4-minute steam.

Curd

Kaya (Coconut Curd)

Makes about 1¾ cups (450ml)

The smell of kaya cooking is a heady combination of egg, coconut and fresh pandan leaves, which makes me seriously giddy with pleasure. It brings back so many childhood memories of being dragged through the smelly, wet markets of Kuala Lumpur, with kaya and a sip of sweet black coffee from an eye-level saucer (that's how small I was) the redeeming part of the day. The Malaysian way to eat it is slathered on toast with thick slices of butter. Don't sweat it too much if your kaya curdles – every second batch of mine seems to but it is still delectable.

5 extra large eggs
500g caster sugar
300ml coconut cream
6 pandan leaves* each torn into thirds
    lengthways and then knotted into
    2 bunches, 3 leaves per bunch

Special Equipment: 1 L capacity heatproof glass OR ceramic bowl/urn with lid + 3 clean tea towels + large heavy-based saucepan with lid + electric cake mixer

Combine the eggs and sugar in a large mixing bowl. Stir the mixture slowly for 10–15 minutes with a clean hand until homogenised and most of the sugar has dissolved. As your hand passes through the mixture, rub the grains of sugar together. The warmth from your hand will slowly dissolve the sugar. Don't be tempted to whisk or beat as you want to avoid incorporating any air into the mixture. Add the coconut cream and mix well, still with your hand. Pass the mixture through a sieve into a 1 L capacity glass or ceramic heatproof bowl with a lid. Submerge the pandan leaves in the mixture. Wrap the lid with 2 clean tea towels layered on top of one another. Gather the sides of the tea towel into a bunch on top of the lid and secure with string or an elastic band (to prevent excessive condensation from dripping into the kaya) and cover mixture.

To cook the curd, begin by boiling a kettle full of water to have on standby. Place a clean tea towel, folded into quarters, on the bottom of a large heavy-based saucepan with a lid. Gently lower the covered heatproof bowl containing the egg mixture into the saucepan. Pour the freshly boiled water into the saucepan, up to 3cm from the lip of the heatproof bowl. Set the stovetop heat on the lowest setting possible, cover the saucepan and cook for 2 hours. Stir mixture every 10–15 minutes to prevent curdling. The result should be a thick silky curd. If the kaya appears to have curdled, quickly transfer it to a mixing bowl and beat on high speed using an electric cake mixer. This will immediately cool the kaya down and improve the texture.

Transfer the kaya into sterilised glass jars**, seal and invert until completely cool before refrigerating. This will keep in the fridge for up to 2 months.

As well as on toast, kaya is delicious on pulut santan – steamed coconut glutinous rice (see page 217). Kaya is also a fab substitute for strawberry jam in Mum's Jam Roll (see page 161).

*Available from Asian grocers. Pandan is available mostly in frozen form and sometimes fresh.
**For notes on sterilising glass jars, see page 219

Blood Orange & Passionfruit Curd

The combination of these two fruits in a curd is fabulous. The curd is incredibly versatile, beautiful on toast and as a filling for a cake or tart.

1 cup (230g) caster sugar

150g unsalted butter, room temperature

4 eggs (you may choose to use
    2 eggs and 2 yolks, which will give
    you a brighter colour)

⅓ cup (80ml) fresh passionfruit pulp

⅓ cup (80ml) blood orange juice and
    zest of 1 blood orange

Special Equipment: electric cake mixer

Beat the sugar and butter with an electric cake mixer in a medium–large mixing bowl until combined. Add the eggs and beat until combined but don't fret when the mixture curdles. Add the passionfruit pulp, orange juice and zest, and beat briefly to combine.

In a heavy-based non-stick saucepan over low–medium heat, cook the mixture, stirring continuously, until it thickens and coats the back of a wooden spoon nicely. Do not allow the mixture to boil or you will split (curdle) the mixture. If the mixture has split (it will look dotty because the protein and liquid have separated), immediately transfer to a mixing bowl and beat on high speed with an electric cake mixer – this will cool the curd down and improve the texture. Transfer into sterilised glass jars*, seal and invert until completely cool before refrigerating. The curd will keep nicely in the fridge for up to 2 months.

*For notes on sterilising glass jars, see page 219

Super Salads

Zucchini & Mint Salad

Feeds 4

This is a simple, refreshing side dish to have with red and white meat or fish. It's a lovely example of how you can easily create interest and variety by altering the texture of a common ingredient just by the way you cut it.

3 medium zucchinis, sliced lengthways
    into 3mm thick pieces
handful of torn mint

Dressing

1–2 tablespoons olive oil
2–3 tablespoons raspberry vinegar
    (see page 32)
1 small clove garlic, peeled and bashed
    (optional)
½ teaspoon caster sugar
salt & freshly ground black pepper

Shake the *dressing* ingredients in a clean glass jar until emulsified. Add salt and pepper to taste, remove the garlic and set aside.

Bring a medium pot half-filled with water to the boil. Cover and turn the heat off. Lay 2 slices of zucchini neatly on top of one another and slice into 3mm wide strands. Repeat until all zucchini is sliced, then drop the zucchini strands into the pot. Wait for 5 seconds before draining in a colander and rinsing with cold water. Allow to drain for 10 minutes more before tipping the zucchini strands onto a clean tea towel and patting gently to reduce any excess moisture. Transfer to a medium mixing bowl, add the mint and combine with the dressing. Mix gently with clean hands and serve.

Suzi's Fresh Beetroot & Chickpea Salad

Suzi, my stylist, brought this in for lunch one day and I fell completely in love with the flavours. It's seriously one of the best salads I've ever had in my life and I always feel terrific after eating it. Pair it with any grilled meat or have it as a light lunch with some tinned tuna.

3–4 small to medium beetroots

1 x 400g tin chickpeas, drained and rinsed

½ continental cucumber, quartered lengthways and sliced into 5mm pieces

1 cup rocket OR baby spinach leaves

¼ cup (60g) sunflower seeds

Dressing

¼ cup (60ml) white balsamic vinegar

2 tablespoons olive oil

½ teaspoon ground cumin (optional)

½ teaspoon salt OR to taste

¼ teaspoon sugar

Special Equipment: disposable gloves

Wearing disposable gloves to protect your hands from staining, peel the beetroots and grate coarsely.

Shake the *dressing* ingredients in a small glass jar until emulsified and the salt and sugar have dissolved.

Combine all the salad ingredients in a large mixing bowl just before serving, add the dressing, toss gently with two spoons and serve.

Fast & Fresh

Neil's Cabbage & Parmesan Slaw

Feeds 4 as a side

This is a brilliantly simple recipe I nicked from Neil Perry. It makes for an excellent side dish to have with any grilled meat – refreshing and decidedly moreish.

250g cabbage leaves with hard stalks and centres sliced away and discarded, shredded as finely as possibly

⅔ cup (60g) Parmesan cheese, finely grated

⅓–½ cup mint, finely shredded

⅓–½ cup flat-leaf parsley, finely shredded

2 tablespoons lemon juice

2 tablespoons olive oil

Combine all the ingredients in a large bowl and gently mix with clean hands. Serve immediately.

28

Blood Orange, Fennel & Persimmon Salad

This is an oldie but a goodie to have as a side dish or light lunch. If you've never tried persimmons before, now is the time – these beautiful orange globes have a mild alluring sweetness and fabulous texture. Shred some chicken breast or crack open a tin of tuna over the top for a healthy meal with loads of refreshing crunch.

2 blood oranges, skins sliced away
   leaving no pith, segments sliced out
   between dividing membranes
½ large fennel bulb OR 1 small one,
   sliced as thinly as possible, fronds
   reserved for garnish
2 sweet persimmons, quartered, stem
   removed, sliced into 5mm pieces

Dressing
2 tablespoons olive oil
2 tablespoons apple cider vinegar OR
   lemon juice
½ teaspoon caster sugar
salt & cracked black pepper
1 clove garlic, peeled, bashed
   (optional)

Shake the *dressing* ingredients in a clean glass jar until emulsified. Taste and adjust seasoning if required, then remove the garlic. Place blood oranges, fennel and persimmons in a salad bowl, pour dressing over and gently mix with clean hands. Garnish with reserved fennel fronds and serve immediately.

There are two main types of persimmon: sweet and original. Sweet ones have a flatter top and are stout like a tomato and best eaten firm and crunchy like an apple, while the original type are more elongated and heart shaped, and can only be eaten when they are completely ripe. The flesh of both kinds will ripen to a jelly-like consistency and can be scooped out of the skin like custard.

Vinaigrette

Raspberry Vinaigrette

These are two of my favourite go-to dressings. Raspberry is common in vinaigrettes but it's simply a platform to bounce off. You can replace it with roughly pulverised grapefruit, pineapple, green apple or mango. Use your instinct to pair with appropriate vinegars, keeping in mind that you don't want the vinegar to overpower or discolour the fruit.

Raspberry Vinegar
Makes about 2 cups (500ml)

1 heaped cup raspberries

¼ cup (55g) caster sugar

1 cup (250ml) red wine vinegar

Vinaigrette
Makes about ⅓ cup (80ml)

2–3 tablespoons olive oil

1 clove garlic, peeled, bashed (optional)

2 tablespoons Raspberry Vinegar

½ teaspoon salt OR to taste

½–1 teaspoon caster sugar

1 teaspoon Dijon OR wholegrain
    mustard (optional)

cracked black pepper

To make the *raspberry vinegar*, combine the raspberries and sugar in a small saucepan and bring to the boil. Stir until the sugar is dissolved then remove from the heat and allow to cool before mixing with the red wine vinegar and refrigerating. This will keep for up to 6 months in the fridge.

To make the *vinaigrette*, shake all the ingredients in a clean glass jar until the sugar and salt have dissolved. Remove garlic before using.

Avocado Vinaigrette

Hilariously, the idea of using avocado as an emulsifying agent came from a TV interview with health-conscious pop starlet Avril Lavigne! The creaminess of the avocado is brilliant for thickening the dressing, helping it adhere to slippery vegetables and making each morsel very flavourful indeed. Simply omit the olive oil for a healthier option.

¼ avocado, mashed

1 tablespoon olive oil (optional)

1 clove garlic, peeled, bashed

3–4 tablespoons lemon juice, apple cider vinegar, champagne vinegar or white balsamic

1 teaspoon salt OR to taste

2 teaspoons sugar

1 teaspoon Dijon OR wholegrain mustard (optional)

cracked black pepper

Shake all the ingredients in a clean glass jar until the sugar and salt have dissolved. Remove the garlic clove before pouring over a salad. This should be made fresh and eaten on the day.

Salty Sweet

Poached Chicken & Pineapple Salad

Using a Somtam dressing, this vibrant salad makes for a perfect light summer lunch – full of seasonal crunch, punch and zing.

Somtam Dressing

110ml freshly squeezed lime juice

2 teaspoons tamarind paste*

2 tablespoons caster sugar OR
  3 tablespoons pale Thai palm sugar*

1–2 cloves garlic, peeled, bashed

1 small red chilli, seeds removed,
  bashed (optional)

¼ avocado, mashed (optional)

Roasted Rice

¼ cup (50g) glutinous rice*

Salad

2–3 chicken breast fillets (depending on
  how much you love your meat)

½ largish pineapple, peeled, centre
  sliced away and discarded, cut into
  5mm batons

½ continental cucumber, halved
  lengthways, seeds sliced away and
  discarded, sliced into steep diagonal
  3mm slices

2 large tomatoes, seeds sliced away
  and discarded, cut into 1cm cubes

½ cup mint leaves, torn

½ cup roughly chopped coriander
  leaves and stalks

½ cup chopped spring onions

Garnish

½ cup (80g) salted roasted peanuts,
  roughly chopped

½ cup deep-fried shallots*

2 long red chillies, finely sliced (optional)

Special Equipment: mortar and pestle OR electric spice grinder

To make the *dressing*, combine the ingredients in a clean glass jar and shake to combine. Allow to rest for 5 minutes then shake again until the sugar has dissolved and set aside.

To make the *roasted rice*, dry toast the glutinous rice in a small frypan over medium heat, tossing or stirring frequently until the grains are golden. Transfer to a mortar and pestle OR electric spice grinder and grind to a sandy consistency. Set aside to cool.

To poach the chicken, cover with water in a small saucepan and simmer, covered, for 10 minutes then turn the heat off and allow to rest for another 20 minutes. Strain the stock through a sieve and freeze for another use. Shred the chicken into thin strands and set aside.

Combine all the *salad* ingredients in a large mixing bowl. Remove the garlic from the dressing, add to salad and toss gently with clean hands.

To serve, divide the salad into bowls and sprinkle generously with the roasted ground rice, peanuts, deep-fried shallots and chilli.

> Roasted ground glutinous rice is used in Thai salads for its impressive crunch factor and also for helping runny dressings stick to salad ingredients. Glutinous rice is favoured for toasting because it's softer and shatters easily when bitten into.

*Available from Asian grocers. To make tamarind paste from scratch see page 219.

Savoury Fruit Salad

Somtam dressing, used traditionally in Thai green papaya salad, is so flavourful and versatile. Making it is a great way to learn just how far you have to push and balance the sweet, sour and salty elements that define the flavours of South East Asia. I came up with the idea of a savoury fruit salad when I was travelling in Malaysia and thinking about how so many Asian cuisines play with notions of sweet and savoury. This is a superb, refreshing salad to have for a light lunch or BBQ accompaniment.

Somtam Dressing

110ml freshly squeezed lime juice

2 teaspoons tamarind paste*

2 tablespoons caster sugar OR
   3 tablespoons pale Thai palm sugar*

1–2 cloves garlic, peeled, bashed

1 small red chilli, seeds removed,
   bashed (optional)

¼ avocado, mashed** (optional)

¾ cup ikan bilis* (Asian dried anchovies)

400ml vegetable oil

Salad

2 heirloom tomatoes OR any ripe
   seasonal tomatoes, sliced into
   small segments

2 firm, not-quite-ripe peaches, sliced
   into small segments

2 green apples, cored, quartered and
   sliced into small segments

1 small Spanish onion, peeled, thinly
   sliced

1 long red chilli, thinly sliced (optional)

½ cup mint leaves, torn

½ cup roughly chopped coriander
   leaves and stems

Garnish

½ cup (80g) salted roasted peanuts,
   roughly chopped

½ cup deep-fried shallots*

To make the *dressing*, combine the ingredients in a clean glass jar and shake to combine. Allow to rest for 5 minutes then shake again until the sugar has dissolved and set aside.

To fry the ikan bilis, heat the oil over medium heat in a medium saucepan. To test if the oil is ready, toss in a few ikan bilis. If they turn golden within 10 seconds, all is well. Deep-fry all the ikan bilis until golden, tip into a sieve lined with paper towel and set aside to cool.

Combine all the *salad* ingredients and ikan bilis in a large mixing bowl. Remove the garlic from the dressing, add to salad and toss gently with clean hands. Divide into bowls to serve and garnish with a sprinkling of peanuts and deep-fried shallots.

> Never store tomatoes in the fridge unless you are chilling the fruit prior to serving – it retards the ripening process and you won't get the best flavour out of them.

> To check the heat of a chilli, cut the stem off and lick it. If you find it is very hot, definitely discard the seeds and pith; if mild use the whole chilli.

*Available from Asian grocers. To make tamarind paste from scratch see page 219.
**Avocado is excellent for thickening any salad dressing because of its neutral flavour and creamy texture which helps dressing adhere to salad ingredients.

Something Wobbly

Crème Caramel

Crème caramel has been my favourite dessert since I was nine and I often requested it from my mum in place of a birthday cake. I can easily wolf down half of this amount in a sitting and have the remainder for breakfast! The traditional French method dictates that it's made entirely of milk, which produces a more delicate texture, but this is my mum's recipe, the one I grew up eating and the one I love.

Caramel

¼ cup (60ml) water
1 cup (230g) caster sugar
2 tablespoons boiled water

Custard

2 cups (500ml) milk
½ cup (125ml) cream
6 eggs
½ cup (115g) caster sugar
1½ teaspoons vanilla bean paste
   OR natural vanilla extract
strawberries, for serving (optional)

Special Equipment: 20cm round cake tin + any largish baking dish that the cake tin can sit comfortably in

Preheat the oven to 140°C or 130°C fan-forced.

To make the *caramel*, mix the water and sugar in a small saucepan until the sugar has dissolved then boil for about 10 minutes OR until the mixture is syrupy and begins to turn golden. The tricky bit starts NOW! I love my caramel slightly burnt because the bitterness adds a lovely depth to the flavour, but you are free to take it to whatever level of colour you like. The window of time you have to make a success of this is small, so you must be attentive or your caramel will go from the most beautiful amber to black and smoking within a second! As soon as the colour you want is achieved, remove from the heat, and, wearing oven mitts for protection, add the boiling water. Stand right back as the sugar mixture will froth up and spit aggressively but it will calm down just as quickly. 'Dousing' stops the sugar from cooking any further and loosens the caramel, so that all of it will release from the dish when you invert the crème caramel – otherwise more than half will stick to the tin. Tip the caramel into the cake tin and allow to cool a little before refrigerating.

To make the *custard*, bring the milk and cream to the boil in a medium saucepan, then allow to cool slightly.

In a medium mixing bowl, whisk the eggs, sugar and vanilla until just combined. Add the hot milk and cream to the egg mixture, mix with a whisk and pour through a sieve into the caramel-coated tin. To create a bain marie, place the tin in a large baking dish and fill the space between them with enough hot water to reach halfway up the side of the tin. Bake for about 60 minutes OR until just set. Remove from the oven and allow to cool completely for about 2 hours before chilling.

To turn out the crème caramel, run a knife around the inside of the tin or use your fingers to gently push and ease it away from the sides, then jiggle the tin gently and you should feel the custard release completely. Cover the tin with a serving plate and turn over in one swift movement. Slice and serve plain or with strawberries.

When I say 'set', look out for what's still a very wobbly texture, however if you can see the liquid rippling under the skin of the custard when you shake the tin a little, the custard needs to be cooked further.

Steamed Egg Tofu with Century Egg Salad

Feeds 4–5 as a shared dish

This is technically not a true tofu because it's not made from soya beans. The idea of calling it 'tofu' is referencing the silken texture that is produced from poaching the egg mixture very gently. This is not a dish for the fainthearted but it's become one of my favourite ways to serve century eggs – it's very traditional Chinese fare, which challenges notions of what's yummy on every level: the texture, the temperature and of course the funk of the notorious century egg or 'dirty egg' as my mate Phil from Liverpool calls it. If you aren't up for the adventure, simply substitute hard-boiled eggs for the century eggs.

Egg Tofu
4 large eggs
1¼ cups (310ml) water

Dressing
3 teaspoons shaoxing rice wine*
3 teaspoons vegetable oil
4 drops sesame oil
1 tablespoon light soy sauce
1 teaspoon caster sugar
1 teaspoon water

2 century eggs* OR 2 hard-boiled eggs, diced into 1cm cubes

Garnish
1 tablespoon finely chopped spring onion
2 tablespoons coriander leaves
1 teaspoon deep-fried shallots*

*Available from Asian grocers. Shaoxing rice wine and deep-fried shallots are available in some supermarkets.

Special Equipment: any porcelain or ceramic vessel that holds 500ml is fine but I found a rectangular dish 10cm x 15cm that was perfect for the job. You need a dish that allows you to run a knife around the edges and use a rubber spatula to free the bottom. So long as you don't care too much about the aesthetics even a basic round bowl will be fine + a pot with lid that will comfortably fit the dish + trivet with 5cm or higher legs

To make the *egg tofu*, mix the eggs and water in a medium bowl with chopsticks by making a slow figure of 8 motion. Pour into a ceramic dish, place on a trivet inside a large pot then cover and steam over the lowest heat possible for about 30 minutes OR until completely set. If the steam is too vigorous the egg tofu will be embedded with lots of bubbles, but this is just a cosmetic issue – it will still taste great! To check if the egg is cooked through, slide a small knife down the side of the dish and see if there is any runny unset egg. If so, steam further and keep checking every 10 minutes. When cooked, allow to cool and then chill in the refrigerator.

To make the *dressing*, combine the dressing ingredients in a small bowl and stir until the sugar is dissolved. Set aside.

To serve, run a knife around the inside of the ceramic dish, then slide a flat rubber spatula snugly against the bottom of the dish, making sure you release all of the tofu. Tip the dish upside down onto a chopping board and trim off any uneven edges. Slice, lengthwise, into 1cm segments, and transfer to a serving plate. Gently nudge the pieces so they lean to one side and sprinkle with the century eggs. Pour the dressing over the salad and garnish with the spring onions, coriander leaves and deep-fried shallots. Serve as an appetiser or as part of a shared main meal.

If the idea of removing the chilled egg tofu from its dish sounds too fiddly for you, simply sprinkle the century egg, dressing and garnish directly into the dish and let the guests scoop out the egg tofu.

Handmade

Abacus Beads

I totally love this dish longtime because it was the dish that granted me that fateful second chance in my *MasterChef* audition. The process is almost identical to gnocchi except in this case kneading the dough is required and the desired texture is slightly bouncy. Its origins are Hakka, my mum's side of the family. Hakkas were a nomadic people dwelling in hilly, unfavourable countryside where taro was one of very few readily available wild ingredients.

Beads

300g fresh or frozen taro*, peeled and
    diced into 2cm cubes
50g glutinous rice flour*
150g tapioca flour*
pinch of salt & pepper
about 2 tablespoons water
vegetable OR peanut oil

Sauce

2–3 tablespoons peanut OR vegetable oil
3 cloves garlic, peeled, chopped
200g minced pork
100g dried shrimp*, soaked in hot water
    for 20 minutes, drained and roughly
    chopped
100g dried shredded cuttlefish*, soaked
    in hot water for 20 minutes, then
    rinsed and drained (optional)
8 large shiitake mushrooms, soaked
    in hot water for 20 minutes, liquid
    squeezed out
2 tablespoons oyster sauce
splash of fish sauce
½ teaspoon sugar
salt and white pepper

Garnish

4 spring onions, chopped
1 long red chilli, chopped
½ bunch of coriander leaves and stalks,
    roughly chopped
2–3 tablespoons deep-fried shallots*

Special Equipment: mouli OR potato ricer

To make the *beads*, place the taro in a steamer and steam for about 10 minutes OR until taro is soft. Pass the taro through a mouli OR potato ricer, OR mash with a fork and pass through a sieve, then cool for about 10 minutes. Combine the flours, salt and pepper with the warm taro mash and knead with a small amount of water until the dough is smooth and pliable. Roll into balls 1.5cm in diameter and gently press each ball between your index finger and thumb to make a dimple on each side. To cook, boil the beads in a few batches in plenty of salted water until they rise to the surface. Drain in a colander and toss some vegetable oil through the cooked beads to keep them separate.

To make the *sauce*, heat the oil and garlic in a wok or large frypan over medium heat and sauté garlic for a few seconds until just golden. Add the pork mince and stir-fry until slightly browned, using a wooden spoon or spatula to break the mince into smaller pieces. Add the dried shrimp, cuttlefish and shiitake and stir-fry for 1 minute. Add the cooked beads, oyster sauce, fish sauce, sugar, salt and pepper and stir-fry briefly to combine. Garnish with the spring onions, chilli, coriander and deep-fried shallots. Serve immediately.

*Available from Asian grocers

Tearaway Dumpling Soup

This dish brings back lovely memories because it was one of the first things my Great Aunty Kim would let me help with in the kitchen. It represents everything I admire about Chinese home cooking: unpretentious, hearty, not particularly attractive but absolutely delicious. When I used to eat this, I knew I was loved.

Dumpling Dough

3 cups (450g) plain flour

1 teaspoon salt

2 eggs, lightly whisked

about 3 cups (750ml) water

4–5 L water

Toppings

1 cup (250ml) vegetable oil

6 cloves garlic, peeled, finely chopped

250g minced chicken OR pork

10 medium shiitake mushrooms, soaked
    in hot water for 30 minutes, stems
    discarded, thinly sliced

2 tablespoons light soy sauce

2 teaspoons dark soy sauce

1 tablespoon oyster sauce

2 teaspoons sugar

½ teaspoon ground white pepper

1 bunch choy sum OR 3 bunches
    bok choy, cut across stalks in half

4 cups (1 L) boiling water

4 cups (1 L) vegetable oil + 1 teaspoon
    extra

1½ cups ikan bilis* (Asian dried anchovies)

2 eggs, lightly whisked

1 portion of Neutral Chicken Stock
    (see page 216)

1 portion of Sambal (see page 219)

Garnish

1 cup chopped spring onions

1 cup roughly chopped coriander leaves
    and stalks

½ cup deep-fried shallots*

*Available from Asian grocers

To make the *dumpling dough*, combine the flour and salt in a large mixing bowl and mix roughly. Make a well in the middle, add the eggs and 2 cups of the water. Bring the dough together, gradually adding more water as needed and kneading until very smooth and pliable and not too stiff. Cover with cling wrap and rest for 30 minutes.

To cook the dumplings, bring the water to the boil in a large pot. Sit your piece of dough on the edge of a clean benchtop and start pulling and stretching the dough away from the bench. As thin areas, roughly the length of your fingers, are stretched out, thrust your hands in an upwards motion then pull away so the tips of your fingers cut out a ragged-edged piece of dough. Immediately drop into the boiling water and wait for it to rise to the surface, then scoop out with a Chinese spider OR slotted spoon to drain in a colander. Continue to do this until you have enough dumplings to feed 5–6. If you want to be certain of an al dente result, plunge the cooked dumplings into cold water before draining.

To prepare the *toppings*, heat the oil in a medium frypan over medium heat and sauté the garlic for a few seconds OR until golden. Leave 2–3 tablespoons of the garlic and oil in the pan and pour the remainder over the dumplings then toss to prevent sticking. Add the minced chicken or pork and shiitake to the pan, increase to a high heat and sauté until the meat is brown, using a spatula or wooden spoon to break the mince into smaller pieces. Add the light and dark soy, oyster sauce, sugar and pepper, then toss to combine and transfer to a bowl. Set aside.

To blanch the choy sum, place in a medium bowl and cover with freshly boiled water. Allow to sit for 10 seconds, then drain in a colander and set aside.

To fry the ikan bilis, heat the 4 cups of oil in a medium saucepan over medium heat. To test if oil is ready, toss a few ikan bilis into the oil – if they turn golden in about 10 seconds, all is well. Deep-fry all the ikan bilis until golden, drain in a sieve lined with paper towel and set aside.

To make the omelette garnish, evenly coat the surface of a medium frypan with oil using paper towel. Heat the extra teaspoon of oil over medium–high heat then coat thinly with the egg. Cook for only a few seconds on each side so the omelette doesn't dry out, then roll into a cylinder and slice thinly. Toss to unravel the long threads, cover with cling wrap and set aside.

To serve, portion into each bowl a cup of dumplings, 2 or so ladles of the chicken stock, 2 tablespoons full of the mince, a sprinkle of the egg threads, a small cluster of the blanched choy sum, a sprinkle of the fried ikan bilis, spring onions, deep-fried shallots and then a teaspoon of the sambal. Enjoy!

Lazy Day Noodle Soup

In terms of speed and convenience, this is right up there with 2-minute noodles for a REALLY lazy lunch or dinner. For this reason I always have the ingredients in the fridge or freezer. It's a dish that my Great Aunty Kim must have made me over a hundred times with slight variations, but Jono and I love it with the unique bounce of fish tofu.

125g dried rice vermicelli or any type
   of dried rice noodle

2 cloves garlic, peeled, crushed

1 tablespoon vegetable oil

2 cups (500ml) Neutral Chicken Stock
   (see page 216)

2 tablespoons shaoxing rice wine*
   (optional)

12 pieces fish tofu*

1 tablespoon fish sauce

8 prawns, shelled, deveined and
   butterflied

6–7 iceberg lettuce leaves, torn into
   smaller pieces OR any Asian greens

a few sprigs of coriander

Cover the dried noodles with cold water and soak for 20–30 minutes, then plunge them into a pot with plenty of boiling water. If you have a thicker noodle you may have to let it boil for a few minutes further but if you are using the very thin kind, dipping into the boiling water for a second will be enough – you want the noodles to retain some bite. Drain in a colander and rinse under cold running water then set aside.

Combine the garlic and oil in a medium saucepan over medium heat and sauté garlic until golden. Add the chicken stock, shaoxing rice wine, fish tofu and fish sauce and bring to the boil, then add the prawns. Simmer until the prawns are cooked through, then remove from the heat and add the lettuce, making sure all the leaves are submerged.

To serve, divide the noodles and soup into two bowls and garnish with coriander sprigs.

*Available from Asian grocers. Shaoxing rice wine is available in some supermarkets.

Roast Duck & Pickled Cabbage Noodle Soup

This noodle soup is brilliantly basic. The hardest part will be sourcing a good roast duck from your local Chinatown. All that's involved after that is boiling!

1 traditional Chinese roast duck**
5 L water
3 x 120g tins Chinese pickled cabbage*
    (sheet choy)
1 teaspoon salt OR to taste
1½ teaspoons sugar
2kg fresh flat rice noodles OR 500g
    dried Vietnamese flat rice noodles
3 long red chillies, thinly sliced

Remove as much of the skin and flesh of the duck as possible and set aside. Place the duck bones in a stock pot with the water and bring to the boil. Reduce the heat and simmer gently for an hour OR until the liquid has reduced by about a third of its original volume.

Meanwhile, using a blunt knife, scrape away and discard as much of the fat on the underside of the duck skin as possible. Slice the skin into thin strips and using 2 forks, OR by hand, shred the flesh into thin strands and set aside.

Pour the pickled cabbage into a sieve, rinse well, then drain and set aside.

When the stock is ready, discard the bones, strain the stock through a sieve and return to the pot. Add the duck skin and flesh, and pickled cabbage and bring the soup to the boil. Reduce the heat and simmer gently for another 30 minutes. Add salt to taste and the sugar.

Place the fresh noodles in a large heatproof bowl and cover with boiling water. Agitate with a fork or chopsticks to loosen and separate the strands, then drain. If the noodles have been refrigerated follow the same process but cover the bowl and allow the noodles to steam in the hot water until they are tender. If you are not using immediately, rinse with cold water after draining. If using dried Vietnamese rice noodles or vermicelli, soak noodles in cold water for about 20–30 minutes, then boil for about 3 minutes in plenty of water OR until al dente. Drain immediately and rinse under cold water to stop noodles cooking further.

To serve, divide the noodles and soup into bowls then garnish with chilli.

*Available from Asian grocers
**Chinese roast duck is available from Chinatown roast meat shops

Blanket in a Bowl

When you're feeling a little lacklustre, boiling a whole chicken can be a big deal. I always have about four litres of chicken stock in my freezer, so when there's a call for a good old-fashioned chicken soup, I'm just a few ingredients and minutes away from wiping those cold weather blues away.

4 cups (1 L) Neutral Chicken Stock
    (see page 216)
1 chicken breast fillet
1 bouquet garni OR 1 bay leaf, 4 sprigs
    thyme, 4 sprigs flat-leaf parsley tied
    with kitchen string (optional)
1 medium carrot, peeled, diced into
    1cm cubes
1 stick celery, diced into 1cm cubes
1 small brown onion, peeled, diced into
    1cm cubes
2 tablespoons jasmine rice OR risoni
salt OR light soy sauce & pepper to
    taste
handful of roughly chopped parsley

Place all the ingredients except the parsley into a medium sized pot and bring to the boil. Reduce the heat and simmer for 5 minutes, then discard the bouquet garni. Keep the soup simmering for about 15 minutes OR until the chicken is cooked through and the veggies, onion and rice are tender. Transfer the chicken to a chopping board and shred by hand OR using 2 forks. Return the chicken to the soup and add salt and pepper to taste. Turn the heat off, toss the parsley in at the very last minute so it retains a vibrant colour and flavour, and serve immediately.

Chinese Chicken Congee

In my culture this is considered the ultimate comfort food. It's the Chinese equivalent of a restorative chicken soup. When we first came to Australia my Great Aunty Kim would make a simplified version of this for me and my brother for brekky but with oats; the purest form of 'fusion' around. This meal can be eaten for breakfast, lunch or dinner and is a great hangover cure.

8 cups (2 L) Neutral Chicken Stock
    (see page 216) OR water
1 cup (200g) jasmine rice, washed and
    drained
2 chicken marylands
2 chicken breast fillets
1cm piece of ginger, bashed
1 teaspoon salt

Garnish

3 spring onions, green part only, finely
    chopped
few sprigs of coriander including stalks,
    chopped
3cm piece of ginger, peeled, very finely
    shredded
⅓ cup deep-fried shallots*
light soy sauce
white pepper
few drops of sesame oil

Combine the chicken stock, rice, chicken pieces, bashed ginger and salt in to a medium pot and bring to the boil. Lower the heat to a simmer and cook for about 30–40 minutes OR until the rice has broken down to form a thick soup. When the chicken is cooked through, remove from the congee and shred by hand OR use 2 forks. Cover with cling wrap and set aside.

Congee may be cooked to several different stages and textures depending on what your preference is. Sometimes broken rice is cooked for long periods of time, so the rice grains completely break down and you get a smooth gruel. My dad loves his very stodgy but I prefer the grains still very evident and the surrounding starch to be watery. If you prefer the latter, the congee must be eaten immediately or the rice will begin to break down from resting or being warmed for too long. Either way, you will find the rice is very thirsty and will keep absorbing the surrounding liquid. Keep topping up with hot stock or water so it doesn't get too stodgy.

Return the shredded chicken to the cooked congee and stir to combine. To serve, spoon 1–2 ladles of congee into a bowl with a sprinkle of spring onions, coriander, ginger, deep-fried shallots, a dash of light soy, a pinch of white pepper and a drop of sesame oil, or have the garnishes and seasonings on the table for your guests to help themselves.

*Available from Asian grocers

Specky Brekky

Bec & Chris's Corn Fritters

My in-laws, Bec and Chris, cooked this for me and Jono while they were visiting from Perth and it's one of the best brekkies I've had. Light and full of summer veggies – what gorgeous, lively flavours to wake up to!

Guacamole

2½–3 avocados
2 tablespoons lime juice
shake of Tabasco
¼ teaspoon salt OR to taste
cracked black pepper

Salsa

4 medium tomatoes, diced into
   7mm cubes
3 teaspoons olive oil
½ cup coarsely chopped coriander,
   including stems
1 tablespoon lime juice
salt, to taste
cracked black pepper

Fritters

1 cup (150g) plain flour
½ cup (125ml) milk
3 eggs
1 teaspoon salt
2 ears corn, kernels sliced away, husks
   discarded
1 small red capsicum, stem and seeds
   removed, diced into 7mm cubes
4 mushrooms, diced into 7mm cubes
½ small zucchini, diced into 7mm cubes
olive oil, for frying

lime wedges, to serve

To make the *guacamole*, roughly mash the avocados in a medium mixing bowl with a fork. Add the remaining guacamole ingredients, mix gently and set aside.

To make the *salsa*, combine all the salsa ingredients in a medium mixing bowl, mix gently and set aside.

To make the *fritters*, combine the flour, milk, eggs and salt in a large mixing bowl and whisk until smooth. Add the vegetables and mix with a wooden spoon until combined.

To cook the fritters, grease a non-stick frypan with 1 tablespoon of olive oil over medium heat. Ladle about 1 cup of the fritter mixture into the pan, spreading the ingredients out and cook until both sides are a deep golden with crispy edges. If you want more crunch, use more oil and shallow-fry. Serve immediately with the guacamole, salsa and lime wedges on the table to share.

Chorizo & Tomato Poached Eggs

If you're looking for something a little 'specky' to cook for brunch on the weekend, this is an excellent hearty meal, full of nutrients and robust flavours.

1 tablespoon olive oil

1–2 chorizo sausages (depends how
   much you love your meat), quartered
   lengthways and thinly sliced

1 medium Spanish OR brown onion,
   peeled, chopped

1 green capsicum, diced into 1cm cubes

1 cup tinned cannellini OR butter beans,
   rinsed and drained

½ cup tinned red kidney beans, rinsed
   and drained

6 x medium tomatoes (720g), skins
   scored, blanched in boiling water for
   5 minutes and peeled OR 700g
   tinned whole peeled tomatoes

1 tablespoon tomato paste

salt and cracked black pepper, to taste

pinch of dried chilli flakes (optional)

4–8 eggs (depending on the individual)

¼ cup flat-leaf parsley, chopped

thinly sliced ciabatta OR sourdough,
   grilled

In a large deep non-stick frypan, heat the olive oil over low–medium heat. Add the chorizo and sauté for about 30 seconds to render some of the fat out. Add the onions and cook until they are soft and beginning to caramelise and the chorizo is crispy around the edges, then add the capsicum and sauté for about 10 seconds. Add the beans, tomatoes and tomato paste and simmer for about 5 minutes OR until the sauce thickens slightly. Add the salt, pepper and chilli and reduce the heat to low. Make 4 holes in the sauce and crack an egg into each hole. If the eggs are sitting very high up on the sauce, use a spatula to push some salsa aside and help the eggs fall into the holes. Cover with a lid and poach for about 7 minutes with the aim of perfectly runny yolks.

Scoop the eggs out very carefully and transfer onto a plate, then cover with foil to keep warm and repeat with the remaining eggs. Divide the sauce and eggs into 4 portions on plates and garnish with parsley. Serve with grilled ciabatta or sourdough slices.

Cheesy Charmers

Cheese Soufflé

I still haven't managed to master the perfect rise with this particular soufflé and even though it is on my dining table frequently, it continues to remain an elusive creature, defying all my attempts to train its sides to be perfectly straight. It definitely rises, but at the very end, just when I think 'I've nailed it this time!' it tends to explode haphazardly like its impersonating a cauliflower. A good thing to remember is that so long as the texture and flavour are correct, that is all that matters.

40g soft unsalted butter

¼ cup (25g) breadcrumbs, crushed to
    a fine powder with a mortar & pestle

60g butter

½ cup (75g) plain flour

400ml milk

1½ cups (200g) gruyere cheese, grated

2 pinches of ground nutmeg

salt and pepper, to taste

6 eggs, separated

Special Equipment: electric cake mixer + large 20–22cm ramekin with 10cm high sides OR 10 small 10cm ramekins with 5cm high sides

Preheat the oven to 200°C or 190°C fan-forced.

Brush a large ramekin OR 10 small ramekins thoroughly with the butter, using upwards strokes on the sides as this will guide the soufflé evenly upwards as it cooks. Pour the breadcrumbs into the ramekin/s, turning and shaking the dish to ensure the crumbs completely coat the butter. Discard excess crumbs.

To prepare the roux, melt the butter in a saucepan over low heat. Add the flour and cook over medium heat for about 1 minute, stirring until the flour and butter mixture become foamy. Add the milk in small portions and whisk until homogenised and thickened. Add the cheese, nutmeg, salt and pepper and beat with a wooden spoon until smooth. Remove from the heat and beat in the yolks one at a time until emulsified.

Beat the egg whites with an electric cake mixer until medium–stiff peaks form. Whisk one-third of the beaten egg whites into the roux mixture, then add the remaining egg whites and fold with the whisk until just incorporated.

Fill the prepared dish short of 1cm from the top. Remove the exposed butter and crumb coating by pinching the rim with your thumb and index finger and running them around the dish – this will help with an even rise. Turn the oven down to 180°C or 170°C fan-forced and bake for 20–30 minutes (about 15 minutes for small ramekins) OR until the top of the soufflé develops a golden crust. The instruction 'serve immediately' is a serious matter with a soufflé as it will deflate in seconds. Although this is usually served as an entrée, I love it with salad or soup as a light main meal.

When working with egg whites, always ensure the whisk and bowl are utterly clean and dry. Also, make sure there is not a trace of egg yolk to be found as the fat content will prevent the egg whites from fluffing up into stiff peaks and instead they will remain a limp watery mess. Egg whites freeze very well, so don't throw them away, portion them into small snap-lock bags for easy handling at a later date.

Cheddar Crusted Apple Pie

I wrote this recipe after an inspiring visit to the King Island cheese factory. It's certainly not an original idea but I wonder how many of you have made or tasted this sensational combination of cheese and apples. A lot of people turn their noses up at the copha content but it does create a wonderful lightness in the pastry that you just don't get if you use all butter instead. If you are feeling adventurous, try using a smoked cheddar.

Crust

2½ cups (375g) plain flour

½ teaspoon salt

100g unsalted butter, chilled, diced into 1cm cubes

90g copha, chilled and coarsely grated

1⅓ cups (170g) cheddar cheese, coarsely grated

up to ¼ cup (60ml) iced water

Filling

1.5kg granny smith OR pink lady apples, peeled, cored, quartered lengthways and cut into 3mm slices

⅔ cup (100g) currants

¼ cup (30g) organic plain flour

⅓ cup (80g) caster sugar

2 tablespoons lemon juice

¾ teaspoon ground cinnamon

¼ teaspoon ground ginger

¼ teaspoon ground nutmeg

50g unsalted butter, diced into 1cm cubes

1 egg, lightly whisked, for glazing

2 tablespoons raw sugar

Special Equipment: 26cm ceramic pie dish + rolling pin + pastry brush

For the *crust*, combine the flour and salt in a large mixing bowl, then add the butter, copha and cheddar. Grab small handfuls of the mixture and rub the fats into the flour until you have a sandy consistency. Add the water gradually and rather than knead, compress and squeeze the mixture so you have just enough moisture to bind the dough into a rough ball.

Divide the dough in half, shape into 2 even balls and squash into thick discs. Cover with cling wrap and refrigerate for a minimum of 30 minutes. Overnight resting or freezing is also fine but you will have to allow for thawing time.

Preheat the oven to 200°C or 190°C fan-forced.

If you enjoy the old-fashioned texture of soft stewed apples, combine all the *filling* ingredients in a medium saucepan and cook over medium heat until the apples collapse but aren't quite tender. Set aside and allow to cool completely. If you're like me and prefer a residual crunch in your apples, the process is much quicker. Combine all the filling ingredients in a large mixing bowl, mix thoroughly and allow to stand for 10 minutes.

Remove the pastry from the fridge and rest for 5–7 minutes. If it still feels hard, give it a bit of a bash with your rolling pin to speed things up. Flour both sides of 1 disc and roll out until 3mm thick. Drape the pastry over your rolling pin and transfer to the pie dish. Lift the overhanging bits and gently pat the pastry into the edges of the pie dish. Trim the sides off with a knife and chill for 20 minutes.

Pour the filling into the pastry-lined pie dish, dot with the diced butter and refrigerate while making the lattice.

To construct the lattice, roll the remaining disc of pastry into a 3mm thick circle and cut into 2cm strips. Begin by using only one half of the strips, laying the longest strip over the centre of the pie. Select strips of appropriate lengths and keep laying them parallel to one another leaving a 5mm gap between each one. Now fold every second strip a little over halfway, back onto itself and lay the remaining half of the pastry at a right angle to the already laid strips. Keep alternating the strips that are folded back and you will create a weave. Work as quickly as possible so the pastry doesn't wilt.

continued over page...

Trim excess pastry with a knife and crimp the edges attractively OR use a fork to press and seal. If the lattice has become very soft from handling, pop the pie in the freezer for about 15–20 minutes. Bake for 15 minutes, then remove from the oven and turn the heat down to 180°C or 170°C fan-forced. Glaze the pie thoroughly with the egg wash and sprinkle evenly with the raw sugar. Return to the oven and bake for 35–45 minutes OR until the crust is a deep golden colour. If you feel the apples need more time and the crust is becoming too coloured, cover loosely with foil and bake for a few more minutes.

Remove from the oven and cool for 10–15 minutes before serving with a warm or churned Crème Anglaise (see page 213).

A Feast with Yeast

Antonio's Pan-fried Pizza

I'm not shy about declaring my deep affection for Antonio. When we first met, he said, 'Do you know, we have something unique in common? My TV career was also launched after coming second in a cooking competition.' This is a precious dish he shared with me in my home, accompanied by lovely memories of queuing up with his siblings at the stove for these 'real' pan-fried pizzas. He said they would quickly scoff down a portion and queue up again until his mama ran out of dough. This pizza truly adheres to Antonio's food philosophy of MOF – minimum of fuss, maximum of flavour.

Pizza Dough

2 teaspoons dry yeast

½ teaspoon caster sugar

about 1½ cups (375ml) warm water

5 cups (750g) Italian 00 flour*

2 teaspoons salt

2 teaspoons olive oil + extra for oiling
   bowl

Sauce

2kg vine-ripened tomatoes

½ cup (125ml) olive oil

6 cloves garlic, peeled, finely sliced

1½ teaspoons salt

½ teaspoon sugar

1 bunch fresh basil, torn

¼ teaspoon freshly ground black pepper

olive oil, for cooking

Parmesan cheese, freshly grated
   (the best quality you can afford)

> This sauce recipe is my own and one I've made in bulk for years. It's very versatile and useful to mix with pasta or gnocchi (see page 215) for a super-quick meal.

*Available from most supermarkets and gourmet stores

To make the *pizza dough*, combine the yeast and sugar in a small bowl. Add 2 teaspoons of the water to emulsify the dry ingredients, then stir in the remaining water. Cover and allow to stand for 10–15 minutes OR until the surface of the mixture is foamy.

In a large mixing bowl, combine the flour and salt. Give it a quick mix with your hands before forming a well in the centre. Add the yeast mixture and olive oil and, using your hand, gradually gather the flour into the centre in a circular motion until all the flour is combined. Tip the crumbly mixture onto a clean floured benchtop and knead until smooth and elastic. Add flour to your dough if it feels too sticky and water if it's too dry. Place dough in a large, well-oiled bowl, cover with cling wrap and let it sit in a warm, draught-free spot for 2 hours OR until doubled in size.

To make the *sauce*, remove stems from the tomatoes and score the skin right round so it divides the tomatoes in half. Place the tomatoes in a bowl, submerge them completely in freshly boiled water using a small plate to weigh them down and leave for 10 minutes. Drain tomatoes, slide skins off and chop roughly. Set aside.

In a medium saucepan, heat the olive oil over low–medium heat and sauté the garlic very briefly until aromatic but not at all coloured. Add the tomatoes, salt and sugar and bring to the boil, then reduce to a simmer for 10–15 minutes OR until the sauce has thickened. When you are satisfied with the consistency of the sauce, stir through a couple of handfuls of torn basil and the pepper. Remove from the heat.

To make the pizzas, heat about 2cm of olive oil in a medium saucepan over medium–high heat. To test if the oil is hot enough, drop a small piece of dough into the oil. If it sizzles right away, it's ready! If your pan is smoking excessively, reduce the heat and wait 2 minutes. Tear off a small fistful of dough, place on a floured benchtop and, with a rolling pin, carefully roll until 5mm thick then lower into the saucepan. Fry on both sides until the dough is puffed up and a pale golden colour, then transfer immediately onto a plate. Quickly spread a small ladle of sauce to cover pizza base, grate a small amount of Parmesan over the top and sprinkle some hand-torn fresh basil leaves. Serve immediately and only make the bases as you go or they will lose their crunch and become leathery on cooling.

Cinnamon Twists with Chocolate Sauce

This is a cheeky little somethin' that I came up with to sate a midnight snack attack. It just so happened that I had a small amount of leftover dough from making Antonio's pizza the night before. You can shape the dough any way you want but I went with a twist because it's perfect to dip into the chocolate sauce.

Cinnamon Twists

¾ cup (115g) caster sugar

1½–2 teaspoons ground cinnamon

½ quantity of pizza dough
    (see opposite page)

1 L vegetable oil

Chocolate Sauce

200ml milk

200g good-quality dark chocolate,
    chopped

Combine the caster sugar and cinnamon in a small bowl, mix, then transfer onto a plate. Set aside.

To shape the *twists*, roll a golfball-sized piece of dough into a 30cm noodle. Holding it at the centre with one hand, use your other hand to twist the dough, pinching at both ends.

Heat the vegetable oil in a medium saucepan over medium heat. To test if the oil is hot enough, drop a small piece of dough into the oil. If it sizzles right away, it's ready! If your pan is smoking excessively, reduce the heat and wait 2 minutes. Lower as many twists as you can fit into the pan without them sticking together and fry for about 10 seconds OR until they are a pale golden colour all over. Drain briefly in a colander lined with paper towel before rolling in the cinnamon sugar.

To make the *sauce*, bring the milk to the boil in a small saucepan over medium heat. Remove from the heat, add the chocolate and leave to sit for 5 minutes before whisking OR stirring until smooth.

Serve cinnamon twists with a warm teacup of chocolate sauce for dipping.

Puff 'n' Stuff

Plum Tarte Tatin

If you find the thought of attempting puff pastry laughable, think again. Rough puff is a simplified version using the same principles but achieved in half the time. And just so you know, watching puff pastry rise is way more riveting than TV! My Plum Tatin method is unconventional because I grew so tired of the puff pastry not puffing properly while the fruit over-stewed into slop underneath that I decided to separate the processes. Doing it this way ensures the fruit is cooked to perfection before turning it onto the already cooked rough puff pastry.

1 portion of Rough Puff Pastry
   (see page 217)

Caramel
60g unsalted butter
½ cup (115g) caster OR brown sugar
generous pinch of salt

10–12 firm plums OR apricots,
   halved and deseeded

Special Equipment: 25cm-base frypan with a heatproof handle

Preheat the oven to 220°C or 210°C fan-forced.

Dust each side of the puff pastry square lightly, then roll it into a 5mm thick circle. Trace around the 30cm frypan and cut a circle out of the pastry with a paring knife. Place on a baking tray lined with baking paper and bake for 20 minutes, then reduce the heat to 180°C or 170°C fan-forced and bake for another 10 minutes OR until deep golden and well risen. Remove from the oven and set aside.

To make the *caramel*, melt the butter in the frypan, then add the sugar and salt. Swirl the butter around to dissolve the sugar and salt, then cook over high heat until the caramel turns a deep amber – I prefer my caramel dark with a hint of bitterness. For more detailed instructions follow the caramel method in the Crème Caramel recipe (see page 40).

Arrange the plums, cut-side down, in the frypan of caramel, in tight concentric circles and bake for 10–15 minutes OR until the plums are just softened but not collapsed.

To assemble the tatin, lay the cooked pastry over the plums and secure by placing a plate large enough to cover the frypan over the top. Wearing oven mitts, invert quickly and be very careful of any hot caramel that might escape. Slice and serve hot or warm with Crème Chantilly (see page 214).

Don't waste pastry scraps! Pile them on top of each other in a uniform shape and gently compress but don't squeeze as this will destroy the layers, then cling wrap, freeze and save for a rainy day.

This is the Big Kahuna of the book – making this dish successfully is a rite of passage for any enthusiastic cook. I've fused and added to recipes by Gary Mehigan and John Torode. The outcome is spectacular flavour and gratification that will keep you beaming with pride for days. However, I will issue a warning that high levels of commitment are required!

1kg beef fillet OR butt fillet (butt fillet is cheaper, slightly harder to handle but will give the same result)

2 tablespoons olive oil

10–12 pieces of thinly sliced Italian prosciutto

1 tablespoon Dijon mustard

1½ quantities of Rough Puff Pastry (see page 217)

1 egg, whisked with a pinch of salt

Celeriac Purée (see page 73)

Mushroom Duxelles

40g dried porcini mushrooms

2 tablespoons olive oil

30g unsalted butter

250g Swiss brown mushrooms, finely chopped

1 clove garlic, peeled, finely chopped

2 red eschallots, peeled, finely chopped

¼ cup flat-leaf parsley, finely chopped

2 tablespoons finely chopped tarragon

2 teaspoons Dijon mustard

150g Chicken Liver Paté (see page 73)

Red Wine Sauce

800g–1kg small beef bones

2 tablespoons olive oil

400ml red wine

2 cloves garlic, peeled, bashed

4 shallots, finely sliced

1 bay leaf

12 sprigs of thyme

150ml port OR Pedro Ximinez

800ml unsalted beef stock

strained porcini mushroom liquid

Beurre Manie (optional)

80g unsalted butter, diced into 1cm cubes

1–2 teaspoons wheaten cornflour

Special Equipment: muslin or cheesecloth + kitchen string + large heavy-based frypan with a heatproof handle + patience and stamina

Preheat the oven to 200°C or 190°C fan-forced.

To make the *mushroom duxelles*, soak the porcini in hot water for 15 minutes. Skim the mushrooms out with a slotted spoon to avoid any grit that might be sitting on the bottom of the bowl, squeeze to remove the excess liquid then chop finely. Strain the porcini liquid through muslin or a fine sieve and reserve for the *red wine sauce*.

Heat the olive oil and butter in a large non-stick frypan over medium heat until the butter is foaming. Add the porcini, Swiss browns, garlic and red eschallots and sauté until soft and fragrant. Remove from the heat and add the herbs, Dijon and paté. Mix well and set aside to cool.

To make the *red wine sauce*, heat the bones and 1 tablespoon of the oil in a large heavy-based saucepan with a heatproof handle over medium heat, caramelising the sides of the bones evenly. Place the pan of bones into the oven to roast for 20 minutes OR until the bones are nicely browned. Remove from the oven, add the red wine and deglaze by bringing to the boil, so any tasty fragments stuck to the pan are lifted. Transfer the bones and wine to a medium–large saucepan, add the remaining *red wine sauce* ingredients except for 6 sprigs of the thyme and simmer over low–medium heat for about 30 minutes OR until reduced by about half its original volume.

Remove the bones, strain the sauce through a fine sieve or sieve lined with muslin into a heatproof bowl, then return the sauce to the saucepan and season to taste. For the *beurre manie*, mix the butter with the cornflour until emulsified, then whisk into the sauce over medium heat until slightly thickened. Cover with a lid and reheat when ready to serve.

To prepare the fillet, stretch the fillet across a chopping board in front of you. If the fillet is fatter at one end, fold the thin end onto itself so both ends are the same size and you have an evenly shaped log to truss. The spot where the fillet is folded can be cut if you want the 2 pieces to sit flatter against one another. To truss, tie one snug loop around the whole length of the fillet then 6 or 7 smaller loops across the fillet. Make sure the trussing is evenly spaced and not too tight or cutting into the flesh too much. Massage fillet thoroughly with olive oil, then sprinkle evenly with salt and pepper.

continued over page...

Heat a large non-stick frypan over high heat and seal the fillet until brown all over. Cool a little before rolling the fillet snugly in a double layer of cling wrap. Twist the ends tightly, then secure with knots so you have a fat sausage. This will help the fillet cook evenly and make it easier to handle. Rest in the freezer for 30 minutes.

Meanwhile, lay 2 generous layers of cling wrap on the benchtop, and on it arrange enough slightly overlapping layers of prosciutto to cover the beef fillet completely. Make sure there is plenty of cling wrap on all sides. Spread the mushroom duxelles evenly over the prosciutto.

Unwrap the beef fillet, snip away the trussing and brush with the Dijon mustard. Place on top of the mushroom duxelles and prosciutto, then roll up as snugly as possible to encase the beef fillet. Using the cling wrap underneath, roll tightly again to make a sausage, twisting and securing both ends with knots, then rest in the freezer for another 30 minutes.

Preheat the oven to 220°C or 210°C fan-forced.

Roll the pastry out into a 3mm thick rectangle, large enough to cover the fillet of beef plus a separate smaller piece for the base – cut this with a 1cm border to allow for shrinkage. Return the larger piece of pastry to the fridge and place the smaller piece on a tray lined with baking paper. Cover the pastry with more baking paper and weigh down with another tray so the puff doesn't rise much and is easier to handle later. Cook for 15 minutes OR until deep golden. Remove from the oven and chill or cool completely before using.

Remove the cling wrap from the beef fillet. Place on the rolled out pastry and cut excess pastry out of the corners so it is in the shape of a thick cross, then wrap the whole sausage up like a present, tucking the edges around the baked pastry base. Carefully transfer the Beef Wellington to a baking tray lined with baking paper. Cut two x 3cm diameter circles out of the cut-offs, place on top of the Beef Wellington, then slice a small hole through the 2 layers of puff to allow steam to vent. Rest in the fridge for a further 15 minutes to chill the pastry before brushing thoroughly with egg. Place in the oven and cook for 40 minutes for rare to medium–rare and 45 minutes for medium. Rest Wellington for 20 minutes before carving and serve with red wine sauce and celeriac purée.

Chicken Liver Pâté

This recipe makes about 1 cup of pâté which is more than you need for the Beef Wellington recipe but any less and it's not worth making. I usually press the remainder into ramekins using a rubber spatula to squish out the air pockets and smooth off the surface, then cover with a thin layer of clarified butter to have with bread or crackers and cheese.

100g unsalted butter

500g cleaned chicken livers (cut off
    and discard any stringy bits and hint
    of green on livers)

2 tablespoons brandy

¼ teaspoon freshly ground black pepper

salt, to taste

generous pinch of nutmeg

2 tablespoons Pedro Ximinez

Special Equipment: food processor OR mouli

Heat the butter in a large non-stick frypan over medium heat until foaming. Add the livers (beware of spitting) and sauté until golden brown on both sides but the centres are still soft and pink. Increase the heat to high and add the brandy. Tilt the pan away from you and light the brandy with a match. As long as you're not behaving erratically your eyebrows will be safe! Return the pan to a flat position and allow the flame to die. Transfer the livers to a food processor and pulverise or mill in a mouli. If food processing the livers, you should pass the livers through a sieve to remove any graininess. Add the pepper, salt, nutmeg and Pedro Ximinez and mix well. Cover with cling wrap and chill the pâté until ready to use. Sealed with fat, pâté can be kept in the fridge for up to a month depending on how carefully it's being handled and stored.

Celeriac Purée

Every time I hold a celeriac in my hand, it strikes me as something a witch from a fairytale might have touched. Don't let this lumpy, unfamiliar character baffle you – once you've peeled it, it will seem less intimidating! As its name suggests it possesses flavour characteristics of celery but the texture is a hybrid of potato and turnip. This purée is great as a lighter substitute for potatoes and goes well with any meat or fish.

2 large celeriac

70g unsalted butter

300ml chicken stock

300ml milk

salt and pepper, to taste

Special Equipment: blender

Peel the celeriac by trimming away all of the bumpy surface with a paring knife then coarsely grate.

Combine all the ingredients in a large saucepan and bring to the boil. Reduce heat, cover and simmer for 20 minutes OR until the celeriac is tender. Allow to cool for 10 minutes then transfer to a blender and blitz in 4 batches. Begin on a slow speed and hold the lid ajar to let some steam escape, otherwise you will have an explosion of hot liquid on your hands! Blend on the highest speed with the lid closed for about 30 seconds per batch to acquire a perfect velvety texture. Season further if required and reheat before serving.

Yummy Curry

Prawn & Pineapple Curry

On a trip back to Malaysia in 2010 while filming for *Poh's Kitchen*, I was lucky enough to work with famous Nyonya cook Florence Tan, and this is one of the many brilliant recipes she shared with me. If you've ever found the idea of cooking Malaysian or using any of these exotic ingredients intimidating, this recipe will allay your fears. Also, watering the gravy down a little and eating it with rice or egg noodles makes for a delicious alternative to a laksa.

Rempah (wet spice paste)

12 small + 5 large dried red chillies*, deseeded and snipped into small pieces

20g belachan*, roughly chopped

3–4cm piece of galangal*, peeled and finely sliced

4 stalks lemongrass, white part only, dry outer layers removed, finely sliced

300g red eschallots OR Spanish onion, peeled and roughly sliced

3 large cloves garlic, peeled and halved

5 candlenuts* OR macadamia nuts

⅔ cup (160ml) vegetable oil

500g pineapple flesh, cut into bite-sized pieces

2 cups (500ml) water

3 pieces dried tamarind*

5 kaffir lime leaves*

350ml coconut milk

2–3 teaspoons salt

¼ cup (60g) caster sugar

700g prawn flesh OR 700g firm fleshed fish

2 tablespoons lime juice

Special Equipment: good-quality blender OR mini food processor

Soak the chillies in ¾ cup (180ml) of freshly boiled water for 30 minutes OR until soft.

To prepare the *rempah*, combine all the rempah ingredients, including the chilli water, in a blender and blitz into a fine paste. Heat the oil in a large heavy-based non-stick saucepan or wok over medium heat and cook the rempah for about 15 minutes, stirring continuously. As the paste caramelises, it will develop a richer colour and become more fragrant and pulpy as most of the liquid evaporates. The rempah is ready when the oil begins to separate from the spice paste. Caramelising the spice paste adequately is integral to a successful curry – the rempah contains many aromatics and the cooking process draws out all the sugars and toasts the spices, turning what would otherwise be a volatile concoction into a wonderful flavour.

Add the pineapple, water, tamarind and kaffir lime leaves to the paste and bring to the boil, then reduce the heat to a simmer for 10 minutes. Add the coconut milk, salt and sugar and bring to the boil, then add the prawn meat and cook for 5–10 minutes OR until cooked through. Add the lime juice, then taste before serving as more salt, sugar or lime may be required to balance the flavours at the end. Although not traditional, you may garnish with mint and coriander.

Serve with steamed jasmine rice and wedges of fresh cucumber just in case your lips need cooling!

> The high oil content in curries helps the rempah or spice paste caramelise properly, so don't be tempted to reduce the amount. If you are concerned about this, you can skim the oil off the surface of the curry at the end of the cooking process.

*Available from Asian grocers. For notes on dried chillies, see page 226.

Beef Rendang

Rendang is definitely one of the most loved beef dishes of Malaysia. There are many regional versions of this dish, but this is the Poh one! In it is a classic rempah or Malaysian spice and aromatic paste, which forms the base for a wonderfully rich, fragrant curry with many layers of complexity.

Kerisik

120g dried shredded coconut

Rempah (wet spice paste)

12 small + 5 large dried red chillies*, deseeded and snipped into small pieces

3 medium brown onions, peeled and roughly chopped

3–4 cloves garlic, peeled and roughly chopped

2½ tablespoons ground coriander

1½ tablespoons ground fennel

1½ tablespoons ground cumin

1 teaspoon ground black pepper

4 stalks lemongrass, white part only, dry outer layers removed, finely sliced

3–4cm piece of galangal*, peeled and finely sliced

3cm piece of fresh ginger, peeled and finely sliced

⅔ cup (160ml) vegetable oil

3kg gravy beef OR chuck steak, cut into 3–4cm pieces

1 cinnamon stick

4 cloves

6 cardamom pods

2 cups (500ml) coconut milk

¼ cup (45g) brown sugar

1 tablespoon tamarind paste*

1½ teaspoons salt

extra brown sugar and salt to balance at the end

Special Equipment: good-quality blender OR mini food processor + mortar and pestle

Soak the chillies for the rempah in ¾ cup (180ml) of boiled water for 30 minutes OR until soft.

To make the *kerisik*, dry toast the coconut in a medium frypan, tossing regularly until it is a deep golden brown. Transfer to a mortar and pestle and pound, in small batches, into a grainy paste. Set aside.

To prepare the *rempah* combine all rempah ingredients in a blender, including the chilli water, and blitz into a fine paste. Heat the oil in a large heavy-based non-stick saucepan over medium heat and cook rempah for about 15 minutes, stirring continuously. As the paste caramelises, it will develop a richer colour and become more fragrant and pulpy as most of the liquid evaporates. The rempah is ready when the oil begins to separate from the spice paste. Caramelising the spice paste adequately is integral to a successful curry – the rempah contains many aromatics and the cooking process draws out all the sugars and toasts the spices, turning what would otherwise be a volatile concoction into a wonderful flavour.

Add the beef pieces, cinnamon, cloves, cardamom, coconut milk, sugar, tamarind paste and salt and simmer uncovered over low heat for 40 minutes, stirring occasionally. Add the kerisik and cook for a further 45 minutes OR until the meat is tender and half the liquid has evaporated. It's really up to you how saucy or dry you want your rendang to be. Taste for balance before serving and add more sugar or salt if required.

Serve with steamed jasmine rice and fresh cucumber.

*Available from Asian grocers. For notes on dried chillies, see page 226. To make tamarind paste from scratch, see page 219.

Wrap It Up

Vietnamese Meatballs with Rice Paper Rolls

Feeds 4–6

This Vietnamese meatball recipe comes from my sister-in-law, Teena, and is now a family favourite. I have altered the recipe a little by substituting the traditionally used tusino curing powder with a mixture of salt, sugar and fish sauce. This makes for a very fun, interactive meal and is surprisingly filling.

Meatballs

1kg fatty pork mince

½ head of garlic, peeled, finely chopped

¼ cup (35g) self-raising flour

1 tablespoon fish sauce

2½ teaspoons salt

1 teaspoon cracked black pepper

130g caster sugar

2 tablespoons honey

vegetable oil, for greasing

Sauce (Makes about 3 cups/750ml)

10 small + 5 large dried red chillies*, deseeded and snipped into small pieces

4 cloves garlic, peeled and sliced

4 red eschallots OR 1 large Spanish onion, peeled and sliced

2cm (thickest part) piece of galangal*, peeled, finely chopped

2 stalks lemongrass, pale part only, discard dry outer layers, thinly sliced

100ml vegetable oil

2 tablespoons tamarind paste*

⅓ cup (80g) brown sugar

½ teaspoon salt

2 cups (500ml) water

2 tablespoons lime juice

100g salted, roasted and crushed peanuts

1 large bunch each of Thai basil*, coriander, and mint

1 portion Basic Chinese Pickles (see page 9)

1 continental cucumber, seeds removed, and sliced OR ½ iceberg lettuce

150g rice vermicelli, soaked in water for 30 minutes then blanched in boiling water

1 packet large round rice paper wrappers (20cm diameter)

Special Equipment: disposable gloves + good-quality blender OR food processor + bamboo skewers

Soak the chillies for the sauce in ¾ cup (180ml) of freshly boiled water for 30 minutes OR until soft.

To make the *meatballs*, combine all meatball ingredients in a medium mixing bowl and mix well with gloved hands. Cover with cling wrap and marinate in the fridge overnight. When ready to cook, roll balls slightly smaller than a golfball, then press gently, so each resembles a fat disc, wetting your hands slightly if they get too sticky. Dip each disc in vegetable oil before allowing it to rest on foil, and don't stress about the fat content as most of it renders out during cooking. After rolling all the meatballs thread them onto skewers for ease of handling and portioning (but this step is not necessary), then grill on a BBQ or in the oven for about 5 minutes each side, turning them to prevent burning. Ideally, you want the meatballs to be brown and ever-so-slightly charred. On a BBQ the meatballs will develop a beautiful smoky flavour but grilling them in the oven is a very convenient option.

To make the *sauce*, combine the garlic, red eschallots, rehydrated dried chillies with the chilli water, galangal and lemongrass in a blender and blitz into a fine paste. To cook the *sauce*, heat the oil in a medium heavy-based saucepan over medium heat. Add the aromatic paste and cook for about 15 minutes OR until the mixture has darkened in colour, thickened and become very fragrant. The oil will have started to split from the paste, which will give it a curdled appearance. Add the tamarind paste, brown sugar, salt and water and bring to the boil. Reduce the heat and boil for 5 minutes before adding the lime juice and nuts. Taste to see if more seasoning is required and set aside.

To serve, present the meatballs on one plate, the herbs, pickles, cucumber or lettuce and vermicelli on another plate and the rice paper wrappers on a third plate. Place two large bowls of piping hot water at the centre of the table. Each diner should have an individual serve of the sauce and a dinner plate. To assemble the rice paper rolls, dip a rice paper wrapper into the hot water for literally a second, ensuring the entire surface is wet. Leaving a space of about 3cm on both sides, arrange across the centre of the rice paper some cucumber, vermicelli, a teaspoonful of sauce, a few leaves of each herb, a few pieces of pickle and 2 meatballs split in half. Fold the bottom of the rice paper over your line of ingredients tucking them in firmly. Fold in the sides, then roll forwards into a cylindrical parcel.

*Available from Asian grocers. For notes on dried chillies, see page 226. To make tamarind paste from scratch, see page 219.

Shredded Spiced Pork & Coconut Relish Pocket

This is a really healthy, tasty fail-proof meal that the whole family will have a lot of fun making. The prep is extraordinarily simple and if you delegate the three components to various family members you will have a superb meal in 15 minutes.

Relish

1½ cups dried shredded coconut

¾ cup (180ml) boiling water

½ cup (65g) pistachios, roughly chopped

⅓ cup coriander leaves and stalks, roughly chopped

⅓ cup mint leaves, roughly chopped

⅓ cup (40g) currants OR sultanas

1 teaspoon honey

2 tablespoons lime juice

pinch of salt OR to taste

Flatbread

2 cups (300g) plain flour

½ teaspoon salt

200ml freshly boiled water

¼ cup (60ml) vegetable oil

Pork

zest of 1 lime

½ teaspoon dried chilli flakes OR ¼ teaspoon chilli powder

1 tablespoon ground cumin

pinch of salt, OR to taste

800g pork shoulder, cut into matchsticks OR firm tofu, cut into 5mm batons

2–3 cloves garlic, peeled, roughly chopped

2 tablespoons olive oil

lime cheeks, to serve

To make the *relish*, combine the coconut and boiling water in a medium bowl, stir until all the water is absorbed, then cover and chill. Just before serving, add the remaining relish ingredients and mix gently with a spoon until combined.

To make the *flatbread*, combine the flour and salt in a medium mixing bowl, making a well at the centre. Pour 150ml of the hot water into the well and stir with a spoon, until you have a rough dough, then cool enough to handle. Tip the contents of the bowl onto a clean benchtop, adding more of the water if required and knead for about 5 minutes, until you have a smooth, firm ball of dough. Roll the dough into a fat cylinder 5cm wide, then cut into 3–4cm portions.

Dust the benchtop with a small amount of flour and squash the portions into flat circles with the palm of your hand, then sandwich pairs of discs together with the oil brushed between them. Dust the benchtop with a good amount of flour and roll the discs into 20cm diameter, 3mm thick circles. Cook in a dry frypan over medium–high heat until each side is blistered with dark brown and black spots. Remove from the heat and pry the 2 layers of bread apart but be careful of the steam. You have cooked 2 flatbreads at once! Repeat until all bread is cooked.

To prepare the *pork*, sprinkle the lime zest, chilli, cumin and salt over the pork and mix with clean hands until evenly coated with seasonings. Combine half the garlic and half the oil in a large frypan over high heat. As soon as the garlic begins to turn golden, add half the pork and sauté until cooked through. If there are any bits stuck to the pan, scrape them up and sprinkle over the pork for a bit of crunch. Repeat the process for the remaining oil, garlic and pork. Divide the pork and the coconut relish between 4 plates and serve immediately with the flatbread.

You can substitute squid for pork and serve with couscous instead of the flatbread.

Uncle Fernand's Paté de Campagne (Pork Paté)

Learning how to cook these French charcuterie classics with my good friend Emmanuel Mollois was like being given treasure. They were taught to him by his now 90-year-old Uncle Fernand who inspired the young Emmanuel to cook. Uncle Fernand was a chef in the Loire Valley and still cooks every day for his family and neighbours. Every time I make these dishes I am filled with gratitude and wonder that I, a Chinese migrant, can share these recipes with my fellow Australians and continue his legacy – thank you, Emmanuel. *Merci, Oncle Fernand.*

250g cleaned pork OR chicken livers
  (cut off and discard any stringy bits
  and hint of green)
1 brown onion, roughly chopped
1.2kg minced pork (shoulder, neck or
  belly)
6 cloves garlic, peeled and crushed
4 eggs
1 teaspoon French 4 spice*
2 tablespoons (40ml) cognac
200ml white wine
25g salt
1 teaspoon freshly cracked black
  pepper
300g caul fat** OR 20 very thin slices
  of streaky bacon OR speck
2 bay leaves
6 sprigs of thyme

Special Equipment: ceramic OR porcelain terrine dish 23cm x 10cm x 10cm OR a similar-sized loaf tin + a large baking dish that the terrine or loaf tin will sit comfortably in

Preheat the oven to 200°C or 190°C fan-forced.

Combine the livers and onion in a food processor and blitz until finely chopped. Transfer to a large mixing bowl with the pork, garlic, eggs, French 4 spice, cognac, white wine, salt and black pepper and mix well with a wooden spoon or clean hands.

Line a ceramic terrine dish with the caul fat, leaving enough overhanging pieces to completely enclose the mince. If you are using streaky bacon, slightly overlap the pieces. Make a pretty pattern with the bay leaves and thyme on the caul fat or bacon, then pile in the mince mixture. Fold excess caul fat or bacon over the mince to enclose.

To create a bain marie, place the terrine dish in the large baking dish and fill the space between them with enough hot water to reach halfway up the sides of the terrine dish. Cook for 1 hour then reduce the heat to 100°C and cook for a further 1½ hours. Remove from the oven and allow to cool.

Invert the terrine carefully onto a plate, then flip it back into the terrine dish with the bottom facing up, so the bay leaves and thyme are sitting decoratively on top. If you feel it's looking a little lacklustre grill until golden brown. For streaky bacon use a cake rack as a weight to prevent the bacon from curling up.

Serve at room temperature or cold with a baguette, cornichons and Dijon mustard as an appetiser or as a lunch or picnic.

*Quatre èpices in French — available from gourmet shops or blend your own (see page 219)
**You will need to pre-order the caul fat from a specialist butcher

Uncle Fernand's Rillettes de Canard (Duck Rillettes)

2kg deboned duck leg meat, with skin, diced into 2–3cm chunks

1 medium–large brown onion, peeled

10–12 cloves

2 bay leaves

6 sprigs of thyme

30g salt

1 teaspoon freshly cracked black pepper

800g duck OR goose fat

Special Equipment: a few small ceramic pots with lids OR clean glass jars with lids OR ramekins

In a large heavy-based non-stick saucepan, sauté the duck for a few minutes over medium heat. Remove from the heat and drain the meat through a colander. It seems a shame to throw this liquid away, so I pass it through some muslin or a fine sieve and freeze in ice cube trays as a basic stock to throw into sauces or stir-fries.

Return the duck to the saucepan over medium heat and sauté until pale golden. Stud the onion with the cloves, cut into quarters and add to the duck with the bay leaves, thyme, salt, black pepper and enough of the fat to cover everything. Cook for 2½–3 hours over very low heat OR 'on one bubble' as Emmanuel would say. Mix with a whisk to shred the onion and meat, then bring to the boil. Allow the meat to cool completely before you scoop it into pots as this prevents the fat from rising to the top of the jar.

Spoon the rillettes into a few small, sterilised ceramic pots. For optimum flavour, refrigerate for 2 days before serving, although it is perfectly yummy to eat right away. If you cover the rillettes with an additional thin layer of duck fat after potting, it will keep for up to a month in the fridge but always serve at room temperature. Serve with a baguette, cornichons and Dijon mustard as an appetiser or as a lunch or a picnic.

Oldie but a Goodie

Steak with Unstingy Mushroom & White Wine Sauce

Feeds 4

'That old chestnut', you might say to the next two recipes, but I'm hoping to give you just a little more refinement than you might get at the local pub. Enjoy!

4 steaks of choice cut
olive oil
salt & pepper

Sauce

2 tablespoons olive oil
50g unsalted OR clarified butter
   (see page 214)
40g or 3–4 red eschallots
2 cloves garlic, peeled and finely
   chopped
10 sprigs of thyme
650g mushrooms, sliced into 5mm pieces
2 teaspoons Dijon OR wholegrain
   mustard
¼ cup (60ml) porcini liquid* (optional)
½ cup (125ml) white wine
⅓ cup (80ml) cream OR crème fraîche
salt and pepper, to taste
¼ cup roughly chopped flat-leaf parsley

Beurre Manie (optional)

1 teaspoon wheaten cornflour mixed
   with 1 teaspoon softened butter

Green Salad

2 tablespoons Dijon mustard
2 tablespoons olive oil
1 tablespoon water
salt and pepper, to taste
1 head of oakleaf OR lamb's lettuce,
   washed and leaves torn into smaller
   pieces

To make the *sauce*, heat the olive oil and butter in a large frypan over medium heat until the butter is foaming. Add the red eschallots, garlic and thyme and cook until everything is soft and fragrant but not coloured. Add the mushrooms and sauté until they are wilted. Add the mustard, porcini liquid and white wine, bring to the boil and cook for about 10 seconds OR until the sauce thickens slightly. Reduce the heat, add the cream and simmer for about 5 seconds. If you feel the sauce needs thickening, stir in the *beurre manie* and cook over medium heat for 30 seconds to 1 minute then taste to check that the flour has been sufficiently cooked out. Add salt and pepper to taste, then add the parsley. Stir and set aside to reheat when the steak is ready.

To cook the steaks, heat a barred cast-iron griddle OR large frypan until smoking. Meanwhile, rub the steaks with plenty of olive oil, and salt and pepper to taste. Depending on the size of the steak and how you like your meat, the cooking time will differ. There are so many methods to gauge the feel but this is mine – the chubby mound of flesh just under your thumb – press that spot to match the resistance on your steak. For rare, cup your hand loosely. For medium, stretch all your fingers and thumb so your hand is flat with small spaces between each. For well done, have all your fingers and thumb outstretched with big gaps between each. Sooooo, I'm just going to set you free on this one!

Resting is the next most important factor and it's simply half of the cooking time. If your steaks were cooked for 4 minutes on each side then rest for 4 minutes. This allows all the juices that have leeched out of the cells to be re-absorbed, keeping the steak tender and juicy. If you don't rest your steaks, all that juice will flow out upon cutting and you will be left with a tough, dry steak.

To make the *salad*, combine the Dijon mustard, olive oil, water, salt and pepper in a small bowl. Whisk, then pour over the lettuce in a large mixing bowl and toss gently with clean hands.

Serve this one how you want. It is an old chestnut after all!

*Dried porcini mushrooms are found in gourmet delis and some supermarkets. To use porcinis, you must soak them in hot water. Instead of wasting the resulting liquid I freeze it in ice cube trays for throwing into sauces or stocks and adding an intense mushroom flavour.

Chicken Schnitzel with Green Apple, Mint & Radish Slaw

This is a base crumbing I've given you here but you are welcome to go wild with it – maybe some chopped nuts, some lemon zest, how about some crushed nori and popped rice? You could swap the slaw dressing with the Wasabi Cream in the Crumbed Oysters recipe (see page 104) and you have yourself a little nod to Japan via ye olde schnitty!

The Schnitty

1½ cups (90g) Panko breadcrumbs*

2–3 tablespoons picked thyme

⅓ cup chopped parsley

⅓ cup (35g) Parmesan cheese, finely grated

1 teaspoon salt

cracked black pepper

4 chicken breast fillets, each sliced into 3, on a diagonal following the length to produce flattish pieces

½ cup (75g) plain flour

2 large eggs, lightly whisked

olive oil, for frying

The Slaw

3 granny smith apples, quartered, cored, cut into matchsticks

4 radishes, top and tailed, halved and thinly sliced

1 large stick celery, thinly sliced

3 stalks of spring onions, finely sliced (optional)

½ cup packed torn mint

Dressing

⅓ cup (80g) sour cream

1–2 tablespoons lemon juice, OR to taste

2 teaspoons honey

½ teaspoon salt

freshly cracked pepper

4 lemon cheeks, to serve

To make the crumb, place the breadcrumbs, thyme, parsley, Parmesan, salt and pepper in a medium mixing bowl and mix. With a rolling pin, bash each piece of chicken between 2 pieces of cling wrap until about 7mm thick all over. Thoroughly dust each piece with flour, then coat well in egg. Press into the crumb mix, coating each side carefully. Gently lay the chicken pieces on a baking tray or dinner plate – it's not an issue to pile them on top of one another.

To cook the chicken, pour in enough oil to reach 1cm up the side of a heavy-based non-stick frypan and heat over medium heat. To test if the oil is ready throw a few breadcrumbs into the pan and if they sizzle immediately and don't burn to a cinder too quickly the oil is ready (Poh's version of 160°C – apparently the ideal temperature for frying). Lower as many schnitzels into the frypan as you can without overcrowding and fry on both sides until golden and crispy.

To make the *slaw*, combine the slaw ingredients in a large mixing bowl, then cover with cling wrap and refrigerate.

To make the *dressing*, whisk the sour cream, lemon juice, honey, salt and pepper together. At the very last minute pour the dressing over the chilled slaw and toss gently with clean hands.

To serve, divide the chicken and slaw onto individual plates with a cheek of lemon on each or pile everything up on shared dishes for your diners to help themselves. DO serve the dressing on the side so the schnitzels stay crunchy for as long as possible. Happy schnitzeling, people!

> A blunt or serrated knife will make fruit and vegetables turn brown quicker so always work with a freshly sharpened one and you will burst less cells along the way. Salt or citrus will also help retard oxidisation – you can sprinkle a little of either over the cut apple but it will still eventually go brown so don't do this too much ahead of time. Fennel can also be treated like this.

*Available from most supermarkets and Asian grocers

As the name suggests this is a real deal Bolognese recipe handed down to my mate Andre Ursini from his Great Aunty Doriana. The first time I tasted this it was epiphanous. I noted with curiosity the use of milk to braise the mince. There's no herbs bar one bay leaf and no garlic in sight. It's a very simple method using common ingredients but the slow reduction of each liquid allows layers of flavour to develop and you end up with a sauce that's packed with richness and intensity. I've paired it with semolina-based silk handkerchiefs, which match the robust sauce, but it is also spectacular with gnocchi (see page 215).

Bolognese

90g butter

4 medium brown onions, peeled, finely diced

2 medium carrots, peeled, finely diced

1½ large sticks celery, finely diced

2 tablespoons olive oil

250g beef mince

250g pork mince

200g spicy Italian sausages, removed from skins

80g pancetta, finely chopped

2 small bay leaves

3 cups (750ml) dry white wine

⅓ cup (90g) tomato paste

3 cups (750ml) milk

3 cups (750ml) Neutral Chicken Stock (see page 216)

Pasta – Silk Handkerchiefs

75g semolina

175g Italian 00 flour*

pinch of salt

2 large eggs + 1 yolk if more moisture is required to bind dough

2 teaspoons extra virgin olive oil

¼ cup flat-leaf parsley, roughly chopped

Parmigiano Reggiano cheese (or best Parmesan you can afford), grated

Special Equipment: pasta maker

Combine the butter, onion, carrot and celery in a large heavy-based non-stick saucepan over medium heat and sauté until soft and very slighty coloured then remove from the heat. Heat the oil in a medium non-stick frypan over medium heat and cook the beef, pork, sausages and pancetta until dry and slightly browned. Transfer to the large saucepan of aromatics and return to a low heat. Add the bay leaves and wine and cook until most of the liquid has evaporated and the surface of the meat is shiny. Add the tomato paste, stir through the meat and cook for another 2 minutes. Add the milk and reduce until a quarter of the liquid has evaporated. Do not stir the pan until the milk has reduced. Cook for 2 hours, gradually adding the chicken stock and gently folding the mixture occasionally. Reduce until the sauce is thickened, then turn the heat off, cover and set aside.

To make the *handkerchiefs*, combine the semolina, flour and salt in a medium mixing bowl. Make a well at the centre and add the eggs and olive oil. With clean hands, use a circular motion to gradually gather the flour into the centre, until you have a rough dough. Tip the contents of the bowl onto a clean benchtop and knead for about 5 minutes, adding a little water or flour if needed, until you have a smooth ball that doesn't stick to the bench. Cover with cling wrap and set aside to rest for 30 minutes.

To make the *pasta*, set the pasta machine on the 1st notch (the thickest setting) and feed the dough through the rollers. Fold the dough into thirds and repeat the process several times until the dough is smooth, flouring it lightly in between rolling if necessary. This is called laminating. Adjust to the 2nd notch, which will roll the pasta thinner again, and then finally the dough should be rolled through on the 3rd notch. Cut the pasta sheets into 10cm squares and place on a floured tray, making sure there is space between each piece, and set aside.

To cook the pasta, bring a large pot of salted water to the boil (using 1 tablespoon of salt per litre of water). Throw a few pasta squares at a time into the pot and cook for 2–4 minutes or until al dente.** Meanwhile, bring the sauce to a gentle simmer. Fish the pasta out with tongs and transfer straight into the saucepan of sauce. Fold the sauce gently over the pasta, divide into portions and garnish with parsley and Parmigiano Reggiano to serve.

*Available from most supermarkets and gourmet stores
**For notes on al dente, see page 132

Spiced Burger with Pumpkin & Caramelised Onion Relish

This recipe was developed during my time filming with Fred's Van in Adelaide, which helps feed the homeless. It turns out that with very little you can make a really yummy, balanced, economically viable meal. If you have little ones that struggle with vegetables, this recipe is a good one to try out for dinner. It is also a good option for feeding the masses without compromising on flavour. If you are intending to cook a decent amount of these, you can make what I call squrgers instead – roll your meat out into a thick slab and simply slice into squares which will save you a lot of time and effort.

Relish

1kg pumpkin flesh, diced into 2cm cubes
¼ cup (60ml) olive oil + extra for
    roasting pumpkin
salt & cracked black pepper
1kg onions, peeled and thinly sliced
¼ cup (60g) seeded mustard
1–2 tablespoons balsamic vinegar

Burgers

2 tablespoons olive oil + extra for
    cooking patties
3 tablespoons ground cumin
3 tablespoons ground coriander
2 cloves garlic, peeled, finely chopped
1 medium onion, peeled, chopped
1kg beef mince
1 carrot, coarsely grated
1 zucchini, coarsely grated
1½ teaspoons salt OR to taste
½ teaspoon sugar
1 teaspoon cracked black pepper
¼ cup (60ml) red wine vinegar
¼ cup chopped basil
¼ cup chopped parsley
1 egg
¼ cup breadcrumbs

10 burger buns
5 iceberg lettuce leaves
3–4 medium tomatoes, sliced into
    5mm pieces

Special Equipment: 10–12cm round pastry cutter + electric cake mixer + disposable gloves

Preheat the oven to 220°C or 210°C fan-forced.

To make the *relish*, arrange the pumpkin in a single layer on a large baking tray lined with baking paper. Drizzle with a generous amount of olive oil and season with salt and black pepper. Toss lightly with your hands before roasting for about 20 minutes OR until the edges are slightly golden and the pumpkin is tender. If the pumpkin appears to be burning or drying out quicker than it is cooking, cover with foil and return to the oven to cook further.

In a large, heavy-based non-stick pot, heat the ¼ cup of olive oil over medium heat and cook the onions until soft and caramelised. Transfer to a large bowl and mash the pumpkin and onions together with the mustard, balsamic and salt and pepper. Mix and taste, then balance with more salt or balsamic if required.

To make the *burgers*, heat the oil in a medium–large non-stick frypan over medium heat. Add the cumin and coriander, stirring continuously to toast the spices until they are very fragrant. Add the garlic and onion and cook until softened. Set aside to cool slightly.

Place the meat in a large mixing bowl and, with disposable gloves on, mix the meat vigorously in a circular motion to work the proteins and get the mince sticky. Tip the mince onto the benchtop, grab handfuls of it and throw it hard onto the work surface for about 5 minutes, then return it to the bowl. If you have an electric cake mixer on a stand, work the meat with a dough hook for 5 minutes and it will do the same job. Next, add the remaining burger ingredients and the cooled garlic and onion mixture and combine. To make the patties, wet your hands and shape the mixture into balls about the size of a large plum, then squash into a 1cm thick disc. If you want perfectly round patties, squash the mince onto a round pastry cutter as a guide.

To cook the burgers, heat a greased large non-stick frypan over medium–high heat, or a BBQ hot plate, and cook the patties on both sides until slightly charred and the meat is cooked through. To assemble, pile a patty, a dollop of relish, a few slices of tomato and some lettuce between 2 bun halves. Then, chomp!

Fish from a Tin

Red Salmon & Dill Tart

This is an excellent midweek no-brainer. Taking the trouble to make the pastry is really worth it because it adds so much more flavour to the dish.

Shortcrust Pastry

250g (1⅔ cups) plain flour
½ teaspoon salt
140g unsalted butter, diced into
    2cm cubes, at room temperature
about ¼ cup (60ml) water

Filling

3 eggs
2 egg yolks
¾ cup (180ml) cream
⅓ cup (40g) frozen baby peas, thawed
⅓ cup (50g) finely grated Parmesan
    cheese
⅓ cup chopped flat-leaf parsley
1 tablespoon finely chopped dill
¼ cup frozen spinach, thawed and
    squeezed to remove excess moisture
2 teaspoons finely grated lemon zest
415g tin red salmon, drained, bones
    and skin removed, flaked
freshly ground black pepper
salt, to taste

Special Equipment: 34 x 10 x 2cm loose-based tart tin OR a round 24cm ceramic tart dish with 3cm high sides

Preheat the oven to 190°C or 180°C fan-forced.

To make the *pastry*, combine the flour, salt and butter in a bowl and rub butter through the flour until you achieve a sandy consistency. Add 1 tablespoon of water at a time, then rather than knead, use a gathering, squeezing action to bind the mixture into a firm, rough ball. Knead just enough to slightly smooth the dough out (or you will activate the gluten too much and destroy the shortness) then roughly shape into a flattened rectangle for a base, or a disc for a round tart. Cover with cling wrap and rest in the fridge for 30 minutes.

Roll the pastry out on a clean, lightly floured benchtop to a 3mm thickness. Carefully line the base and sides of your tart dish and blind bake for 10–15 minutes OR until a very light golden colour.

Meanwhile, combine all the *filling* ingredients in a medium mixing bowl and mix with a fork. Pour into the tart shell and bake for 20 minutes OR until cooked through. If you are unsure, insert a knife into the centre and have a peek. Serve with salad for a gorgeous light meal.

Tuna & Herb Rice

This is another old faithful I love to make on the days I refuse to leave the house. It's a dish I endearingly call one of my 'binner' specials because it salvages any wilting herbs, slightly wrinkly tomatoes and leftover rice, transforming them into the yummiest, healthy one-pot meal.

2 tablespoons olive oil

2–3 teaspoons cumin seeds

2 teaspoons ground coriander

1–2 cloves garlic, peeled and finely
　　chopped

1 large brown or Spanish onion, peeled,
　　diced into 5mm cubes

½ teaspoon dried chilli flakes

pinch of salt

425g tin tuna, drained thoroughly and
　　flaked

1 cup (185g) cooked jasmine OR
　　basmati rice

2–3 medium vine-ripened tomatoes,
　　diced into 1cm cubes

⅓ cup chopped coriander, including
　　stalks

⅓ cup chopped mint leaves

⅓ cup chopped parsley

cracked black pepper

light soy sauce to taste

In a large non-stick frypan, heat the oil over medium heat with the cumin seeds and coriander until spices are fragrant and foaming. Add the garlic, onion, chilli and salt and sauté until onion is tender. Add the tuna and rice and cook until heated through. Remove from the heat, add the tomatoes, all your chopped herbs and some pepper. Mix or toss until combined, season with the soy and serve immediately.

Mouthwatering Molluscs

Stir-fried Cockles with Brown Bean & Ginger Sauce

Feeds 2–4 as a shared meal

I came up with this recipe after an inspiring canoe trip down the Coorong in South Australia with my friend Brenton Cowell. The cockles from these parts are unbeatable in their sweetness and, truly, I could have eaten a mountain of them just steamed in their own juices, but if you want to add a versatile stir-fry to your repertoire, you must try this one. The brown bean sauce is fabulous with just about any seafood – mussels, squid, prawns, crab or scallops.

1kg pipis, cockles or shellfish of your choice
2–3 tablespoons vegetable oil
3 cloves garlic, peeled, finely chopped
2–3 tablespoons finely shredded ginger
1 long red chilli, finely chopped
2 tablespoons brown beans*, rinsed in cool water, drained and chopped
½ cup chopped spring onions
2 tablespoons shaoxing rice wine
¼ teaspoon sugar

Soak the cockles in a bowl of water to remove residual grit. When draining the cockles, gather handfuls of them and transfer to a colander. If you pour the cockles into the colander you will be pouring the expelled grit back over them. Rinse and refrigerate if not using immediately.

Combine the oil, garlic and ginger in a wok or large frypan and sauté over medium–high heat until lightly coloured. Add the chilli, brown beans and spring onion and stir-fry for 30 seconds. Add the cockles, shaoxing and sugar, toss to coat the cockles in the sauce and stir-fry until all the shells are open. If the cockles won't open, cover the wok for 1–2 minutes to trap them in more steam and stop the pan juices from evaporating. Discard any cockles that do not open. Remove from the heat, plate and serve with steamed jasmine rice.

To check the heat of a chilli, cut the stem off and lick it. If you find it is very hot, definitely discard the seeds and pith. If mild use the whole chilli.

*Brown beans, available from Asian grocers, are usually packaged in a glass jar and most commonly come in two forms: whole beans in a runny sauce or brown bean paste in which the beans are blended into the sauce. It is best to use the whole form because the flavour is better and you can easily remove some of the salt content by rinsing the beans in cold water and draining them in a sieve.

Mussels with Tomato & White Wine

Seriously, nothing beats white wine with mussels. Nothing. Whenever I have my family around for dinner, this is the recipe that gets the most requests and when I was in France I ordered moules frites just about every second meal I ate.

1.5kg tomatoes
100ml olive oil
3 cloves garlic, peeled and finely sliced
1¼ cups (310ml) white wine
2kg mussels, cleaned and bearded
½ cup roughly chopped flat-leaf parsley
    including stalks
cracked black pepper OR dried
    chilli flakes
1 rustic loaf, to serve

To peel the tomatoes, remove the stems and score around the middle of each tomato. Place the tomatoes in a pot or bowl and submerge them completely with freshly boiled water then weigh them down with a small plate and leave for 15 minutes. Drain and rinse with cold water before handling and the skins should slide off with ease. Roughly chop and set aside.

To cook the mussels, heat the olive oil and garlic in a large pot over medium heat and sauté until the oil is fragrant but the garlic is not coloured. Add the tomatoes and simmer for about 10 minutes then add the white wine and bring to the boil for 1 minute. Add the mussels, cover and cook until all the shells are open. Remove from the heat and add the parsley and pepper OR chilli flakes. Serve immediately in bowls with a rustic loaf to mop up the juices.

If you can't find ready-cleaned bearded mussels, tip all your mussels into a clean sink, scrub the shells roughly with a scourer or hard-bristled brush, remove the beards and rinse under cold water. Ease the beards away rather than use an abrupt motion or you might snap the beards and leave remnants behind. Refrigerate until needed.

Shellfish Wasabi

Crumbed Oysters with Wasabi Cream

Feeds 4–6 as a starter

For those who find this slippery little mollusc a little dubious, fear not, for here we have some crunch and a lovely creamy sauce to go with it. I once cooked this by the beach with many naysayers watching on but the outcome surprised even me. By sunset, the crumbed oyster slathered in wasabi cream had gained a legion of fans. Please, do try – ESPECIALLY if this isn't your thing!

Wasabi Cream

1 cup (250g) crème fraiche OR sour cream

1–2 teaspoons wasabi, to taste

2 tablespoons lime juice

¼ teaspoon salt, OR to taste

2 teaspoons caster sugar

Oysters

2 dozen freshly shucked oysters

½ cup (75g) plain flour

1 egg, lightly whisked

1 cup (60g) Panko breadcrumbs*

2 cups (500ml) vegetable oil

rock salt, for serving

2 tablespoons chives, finely chopped

2 tablespoons tobiko* (orange flying fish roe)

icing sugar, for dusting

1 lime, cut into small wedges (optional)

Special Equipment: Chinese spider

To make the *wasabi cream*, whisk the crème fraîche in a medium mixing bowl until medium peaks form. Mix the remaining wasabi cream ingredients in a small bowl before adding to the crème fraîche. Stir gently with the whisk until emulsified. Taste and adjust the seasoning with more salt or sugar if required.

Remove the *oysters* from the shells and lay them on a double layer of paper towel. Pat dry with more paper towel, then roll them gently in the flour making sure all surfaces are thoroughly covered or the egg won't stick. Coat carefully in the egg, then roll in the breadcrumbs, pressing gently so the crumbs stick.

Heat the oil in a small saucepan over high heat. To test if the oil is ready, dip a wooden chopstick or wooden spoon into the oil. If a flurry of small bubbles appears, the oil is ready. Test-fry 1 oyster – it should brown in literally 2 seconds, any longer and you will overcook the oysters. Fry the oysters for about 4 seconds, in batches of 4 or 5 – they should turn golden brown almost instantly. Immediately scoop them out with a Chinese spider and transfer onto some paper towel to drain the excess oil.

To serve, arrange the oyster shells on a platter covered generously with rock salt. Dollop a teaspoonful of wasabi cream into the empty shells then sprinkle some chopped chives and tobiko on top. Dust a small amount of icing sugar over the fried oysters (don't doubt this, it's fab) and perch them on the top edge of the shell so that they are not touching the wasabi cream and serve immediately with lime wedges.

Créme fraîche is a cultured cream that tastes very similar to sour cream but is more luscious and has more character – it also has the advantage of being able to be whipped unlike sour cream which is lighter and turns watery when whisked. You can use sour cream here but the sauce will end up a little runny. If you want to make your own créme fraîche, see page 215.

*Available from Asian grocers. Tobiko is found in the freezer section at Asian grocers.

Seared Scallops with Green Apple & Wasabi Cream

This is a lovely starter that never fails to impress but requires very little effort. The richness of the scallop meat with the sweet crunch of green apple and piquancy of the wasabi cream make for a beautifully balanced bite.

12 large scallops (more if they are small)

2 tablespoons olive oil

30g unsalted butter OR omit olive oil and use 40g clarified butter instead (see page 214)

½ portion of Wasabi Cream (see opposite page)

1 small Granny Smith, quartered, core removed, cut into matchsticks

Lay the scallops on a double layer of paper towel, then pat dry with more paper towel.

Combine the olive oil and butter in a heavy-based non-stick pan over medium–high heat until the butter is foaming, then quickly arrange the scallops in the pan, leaving space between them so they don't overcrowd, and steam. Cooking these on the BBQ is also an excellent option. Cook for about 30 seconds–1 minute, depending on size. You want some nice caramelisation on at least one side and the best way to check if they are cooked is to give them a prod. Just like all meat, you want just the right amount of resistance and yes, it is a bit of a Goldilocks situation but the best way to learn is from experience – squidgy is under-done, hard is overdone, you want something in between. Also don't forget that when you're dealing with such a small morsel, residual heat can be your friend or enemy.

To serve, be as creative as you like. I usually pipe or dollop about a teaspoon of wasabi cream on the top or at the base of each scallop then arrange a teepee shaped pile of apple on top. Serve immediately as a canapé or entree.

A blunt or serrated knife will make fruit and vegetables turn brown quicker so always work with a freshly sharpened one and you will burst less cells along the way. Salt or citrus will also help retard oxidisation – you can sprinkle a little of either over the cut apple but it will still eventually go brown so don't do this too much ahead of time. Fennel can also be treated like this.

Snapper Jacket

Crispy Leatherjackets with Red Eschallot & Chilli Relish

This is a classic Great Aunty Kim recipe – simple but packed full of flavour. Incidentally, it's also a very Malay way to eat. In the modest self-sufficient kampungs much of your food would be gathered from the garden and the protein would usually come in the form of dried or cured seafood or from small fresh fish, collected from nearby ponds, streams or the sea. The accompaniments are always meagre but their highly concentrated flavours are designed to give life to the rice, which is the centre of each meal.

1kg leatherjackets, tommy ruffs, mullet
   or small sardine fillets
1 cup wheaten cornflour or tapioca
   starch*
2 cups (500ml) vegetable oil

Chilli Relish

½ cup (125ml) lime juice
¼ cup (55g) sugar
¼ cup (60ml) light soy sauce
1 tablespoon dark caramel soy sauce*
150g red eschallots, peeled, sliced as
   thinly as possible
2–3 red chillies, seeds removed, finely
   chopped

Combine all the *relish* ingredients except the eschallots and chillies in a medium mixing bowl and stir until the sugar has dissolved. Add the eschallots and chillies 10–15 minutes before serving and mix well.

To prepare the fish, dust the fillets thoroughly with the cornflour. Heat the oil in a medium–large heavy-based non-stick frypan over medium heat. To test if the oil is hot enough, dip a wooden chopstick or wooden spoon into the oil. If a flurry of bubbles rises to the surface, the oil is ready. Fry one piece of fish at a time, turning on both sides until the fillets are golden brown and very crispy. Rest in a colander lined with plenty of paper towel until ready to eat.

Serve hot or at room temperature with the relish and steamed jasmine rice.

*Available from Asian grocers

Steamed Tiew Chew Fish (Snapper)

Feeds 2–4 as a shared dish

This is definitely one of my favourite home-cooked fish dishes. It has that unique Chinese habit of mixing meats which is not seen as much in Western styles of cooking. The pork belly sweetens the cooking juices from the fish and the piquancy of the tomato, pickled mustard and sour plums makes for an intriguing and beautifully balanced dish.

Fish

1 baby snapper, cleaned and scaled

1 tablespoon shaoxing rice wine*

½ teaspoon caster sugar

dash of white pepper

Sauce

5 medium shiitake mushrooms

80g pork belly, thinly sliced

3–4 leaves pickled mustard stem*,
    sliced into 5mm shreds

200g silken tofu*, diced into 2cm cubes

2 pickled plums*, deseeded and
    squashed

1 medium tomato, cut into 8–10 wedges

1 tablespoon fish sauce OR to taste

1 teaspoon soy

½ teaspoon caster sugar

white pepper

2–3 tablespoons finely shredded ginger

Special Equipment: wok with a domed lid + steaming trivet with 3cm high legs + 25–30cm heatproof dish with 4cm high sides + a largish ceramic tart dish

Soak the shiitake mushrooms for the sauce in hot water for 40 minutes OR until soft, then squeeze to remove excess moisture. Discard stems and slice caps thinly.

Score the flesh of the fish to the bone at 2cm intervals – 3 times on each side. Rub the shaoxing, sugar and pepper all over the fish and marinate for 10 minutes.

Place the fish in a heatproof dish and spread the *sauce* ingredients around the dish, finishing with the ginger sprinkled directly over the fish. Place the dish on a steaming trivet and steam covered in a wok with a domed lid over high heat for 10–20 minutes OR until the fish is perfectly cooked. Halfway through, baste the fish with the surrounding juices. If you are unsure whether the fish is cooked, make a very small incision at the fattest part of the fish and gently pry apart the flesh to check. If the flesh closest to the bone is the tiniest bit translucent, it is ready. Remove the wok from the heat, keeping the fish covered and the residual heat will finish off the cooking. Serve with steamed jasmine rice as a shared dish.

Bream or baby barramundi are good alternatives or fillets of your favourite fish if you are too scared to go for a whole one.

*Available from Asian grocers. Silken tofu is available from most supermarkets.

Raw

Tuna & Nashi Carpaccio with Mandarin Dressing

This dish was inspired by a trip to Port Lincoln in South Australia where I had the pleasure of sharing some ocean space with some very handsome tuna – a wonderfully surreal experience to feel their plump bodies zipping by and brushing up against my skin. I wanted to design a raw, modern dish that drew subtly on Asian flavours.

1 tablespoon lemon juice

1½ nashi pears, peeled, cored, quartered and sliced into 2mm pieces

360g sashimi-grade tuna OR kingfish fillets, sliced into 3mm thick pieces

Dressing

¼ cup (60ml) grapeseed oil

3–4 tablespoons fresh mandarin juice

zest of ½–1 mandarin

2 teaspoons verjuice (optional)

2 teaspoons light soy

¼ teaspoon grated ginger

¼ teaspoon finely chopped garlic

salt to taste

Garnish

½ teaspoon black smoked sea salt OR regular sea salt flakes

3 tablespoons continental cucumber, seeds removed, diced into 2mm pieces

2 teaspoons red eschallots, diced into 2mm pieces

1 tablespoon finely chopped parsley

1 tablespoon torn coriander leaves OR chervil

¼ teaspoon freshly crushed Szechuan pepper*

*Available from Asian grocers

Combine all the *dressing* ingredients in a clean glass jar and shake until emulsified, then set aside.

Sprinkle the lemon juice over the nashi and gently toss to prevent the sliced pear from oxidising. Drain the nashi if there is excess liquid. Divide into 4 portions and arrange the slices in a concentric pattern at the centre of each plate. Divide the tuna into 4 portions and arrange in a concentric pattern over the nashi pear. Spoon the dressing over the fish making sure the surface is thoroughly covered and has a glossy surface.

Sprinkle each *garnish* item evenly over the surface of the fish. Serve immediately, on its own or with some bread. Another option is to plate all four serves on a platter to share at the centre of the table which usually makes the portions stretch further.

Patty's Salmon Carpaccio with Capsicum, Caper & Chilli Oil

Feeds 4 as a starter

. . . .

The first time I tasted this dish, I was struck by the quality of the olive oil and clever use of the very simple seasonal ingredients. It is the work of Patty Streckfuss, a Jamie Oliver *Fifteen* success story, and now at 23 the head chef of Andre's Cucina, Adelaide. When I asked Patty where the dish came from, she said, 'I just wanted to use beautiful colours to make an attractive, tasty summer dish.' Buttery salmon aside, I could drink this infused oil – it's so wonderfully balanced with the sweetness of capsicums, salt from the capers and a lovely astringency from the white balsamic. If you have some leftover oil, it keeps very well and is perfect to have with grilled meat or in salads. It is best to make the dressing the night before, so the flavours are well infused.

360g salmon fillets, without skin
sea salt flakes
cracked black pepper
extra-virgin olive oil, for finishing
2 tablespoons picked chervil
2 tablespoons chopped parsley

Dressing

½ cup (80g) mixed red, green, yellow
   capsicum, finely diced
1 tablespoon long red chilli, seeds
   removed, finely diced
2 tablespoons capers, finely chopped
1 clove garlic, peeled, finely chopped
⅓ cup (80ml) good-quality olive oil
⅓ cup (80ml) white balsamic vinegar
salt & pepper, to taste

Mix all the *dressing* ingredients together in a small mixing bowl, cover with cling wrap and allow it to sit overnight or 1–2 hours minimum.

Slice the salmon as thinly as possible – on an angle is easier. Arrange the salmon slices on a single platter or individual plates so that the pieces only slightly overlap and there are no gaps between the fish. Season carefully with sea salt flakes and cracked pepper, then cover the fish thoroughly with the dressing. Drizzle the olive oil over the top to immerse the fish and give the surface a lovely gloss, then garnish with the chervil and parsley. Serve immediately as is or with slices of toasted ciabatta.

Love Hate

Anchovy Butter

Compound butters are *the* most useful things when you want to slap something on the BBQ but you want an instant sauce that's a bit more posh than say mustard or ketchup – not that there's anything wrong with those. You can have a lot of fun and make your own butters with the addition of things like olives, nuts, dried spices and fruit.

125g unsalted butter, room temperature

6–8 anchovy fillets, finely chopped

¼ cup roughly chopped parsley

2 tablespoons capers OR caperberries, roughly chopped

zest of ½ lemon

¼ teaspoon freshly ground black pepper

½ teaspoon sea salt flakes

Combine all the ingredients in a medium mixing bowl and stir well. Dollop dessertspoons of the mixture along a double layer of cling wrap 25cm long. Take the edge closest to you, pull it over the line of butter and tuck it into the open side of the cylinder. If the butter is not nicely distributed, give it a bit of a squish here and there to even the mixture out, then roll up. To finish, twist both ends at the same time like a lolly wrapper and hopefully this will force the butter into a beautiful, evenly shaped sausage. Knot the ends to secure and refrigerate or freeze. If you don't plan on using the whole log in one hit, omit the parsley and freeze the lot.

To use, cut a disc from the log and pop onto a piping hot piece of steak. The compound butter will melt and give you an instant sauce with oodles of personality.

Bagna Cauda

Bagna cauda is a Piedmontese dish and a favourite of mine. I was first introduced to the idea of this dish by my friend and restaurateur Andre Ursini, but this recipe is Antonio Carluccio's. If you're not a fan of this salty little fish, now's the time to try it because there are few other dishes that give it such an elaborate dressing-up and there is no better way to eat raw seasonal vegetables. Even my lovely Jono likes this when usually he wouldn't touch an anchovy with a ten-foot pole.

Crudités

1 yellow capsicum

1 red capsicum

1 green capsicum

1 fennel bulb, fronds reserved for
  garnish

12 cauliflower florets

4 sticks celery

8 radishes

3 carrots

Bagna Cauda

16 cloves garlic, peeled

milk

30 small anchovy fillets, drained

300g good quality unsalted butter

200ml extra virgin olive oil

100ml cream (double cream if you want
  to be naughty)

fresh or toasted slices of ciabatta
  (optional)

Special Equipment: blender OR stick blender

To prepare the *crudités*, cut all the vegetables into irregular shapes which you imagine will be useful for scooping. For root vegetables I like to roll and slice on a steep diagonal and for veggies with a flattish surface like capsicum cut into elongated triangles. For cauliflower, slice the florets not too thinly, so you have flat trees. The fennel will oxidise quickly so cut at the last minute and use a sharp knife. If you are hellbent on being prepared to the max, slice ahead of time and toss the fennel in some lemon juice, but this will only buy you more time, it won't stop it from going brown altogether.

To make the *bagna cauda*, place the garlic in a small saucepan and cover with just enough milk. Cook over very low heat for about 20 minutes OR until the garlic is completely soft. Remove from the heat and crush the garlic into the milk with a fork. Add the anchovies and return to a low heat, stirring until they are dissolved, then blitz with a blender OR stick blender until smooth. Add the butter and olive oil and stir until combined, then stir in the cream.

To serve, portion the bagna cauda into individual pots or in a single larger fondue dish at the centre of the table with a candle underneath to keep it warm. The vegetables can also be portioned out or scattered beautifully onto a communal platter. Then it's simply a matter of dipping and mopping the remainder up with the bread, but between you and me, I'd happily drench a steak with the leftovers.

> If you can find and afford heirloom or baby vegetables, these will add interest and an ornamental touch to the dish. Also, the vegetables I've chosen are just a guide, by all means do your own thing as long as seasonality is king.

Hainanese Chicken Rice

If you are a lover of chicken and comfort food, I doubt you will find another dish that celebrates both quite so thoroughly. As well as the traditional ginger and spring onion sauce, Malaysians also serve it with a garlic chilli sauce and kecap manis, a sweet, sticky soy. It's such a simple meal to make and if you don't count the poaching time it only takes 20 minutes to put together.

The Chook

1.5kg whole chicken
1 clove garlic, bashed
3cm piece of ginger, sliced and bashed
5 spring onions, knotted together
2 tablespoons shaoxing rice wine*
2 tablespoons light soy
1 teaspoon sesame oil
1 teaspoon salt

1 tablespoon light soy
3 teaspoons sesame oil

Rice

2 tablespoons vegetable OR peanut oil
2 cloves garlic, peeled, finely chopped
2 slices of ginger, 5mm thick, bashed
3 cups (600g) jasmine rice, washed,
    drained in a sieve
1 teaspoon salt
1 pandan leaf*, fresh or frozen
4½ cups (1.125 L) chicken stock, from
    poaching chicken

Red Sauce

3–4 long red chillies, roughly sliced
3 cloves garlic, peeled, roughly sliced
⅓ cup (80ml) white vinegar
⅓ cup (80g) caster sugar
½ teaspoon salt

Green Sauce

8 stalks spring onions, finely sliced
6–7cm ginger, peeled, finely grated
2 teaspoons salt
⅓ cup (80ml) vegetable OR peanut oil

sliced cucumber
1 spring onion, finely sliced
1 tablespoon deep-fried shallots*
¼ cup (60ml) kecap manis*

Cut the fat surrounding the inner part of the chicken cavity away and reserve for the rice. Stuff all the *Chook* ingredients into the cavity of the chicken and secure the opening with a short skewer. Lower the chicken into a stock pot that fits it snugly around the sides but is tall enough to allow the chicken to be covered with water. Bring to the boil, cover, and reduce the heat to poach it very gently for 1 hour, so that there is only a slow steady stream of bubbles. Skim any frothy impurities and oil off the surface of the stock as it cooks.

Meanwhile, prepare the rub by mixing the soy and sesame oil in a small bowl. To test if the chicken is cooked, lift it by one of the legs and if it pulls away easily where the thigh joins the body it is done. Transfer the bird onto a plate and massage with the rub. Cover and set aside, then bring the stock back to the boil. Boil for 1 hour OR until you've reduced the stock by one-third (you'll need at least 2.5 L left).

To cook the *rice*, heat the oil and reserved chicken fat in a large non-stick saucepan over medium heat. When the pieces of fat have shrunk considerably, add the garlic and ginger and sauté until fragrant and slightly golden. Add the rice and stir to toast the grains for a few seconds. Add the salt, pandan and chicken stock, stir and bring to the boil. Reduce to a simmer, cover and cook for about 10 minutes OR until the surface is dotted with pits and no liquid is visible. Reduce to the lowest heat and cook for another 10 minutes, then turn the heat off and rest for 15 minutes before uncovering and fluffing with a fork. Cover and set aside.

Blitz all the *red sauce* ingredients with a blender OR stick blender until smooth. If using a mortar and pestle, pound the chilli and garlic in small amounts, then mix with the vinegar, sugar and salt. Refrigerate.

To make the *green sauce*, combine spring onions, ginger and salt in a bowl then sit it in the sink. Heat oil in a small saucepan over high heat until smoking – stand back while you pour it over the aromatics to avoid spitting oil. Mix and set aside.

To serve, debone chicken and slice into 2cm pieces, then divide chicken and cucumber between 4 dinner plates. Pour about 1 cup of broth into 4 individual bowls and garnish with the sliced spring onions and deep-fried shallots. Press about 1 cup of rice into a small rice bowl, then invert onto individual dinner plates. Divide all the sauces and the kecap manis into small dishes so everyone has their own. Don't hold back on the sauces when you are eating this meal. Because the chicken is subtly flavoured, all the seasoning comes in the form of the sauces. Make sure you put a little of each in every spoonful.

*Available from Asian grocers

Nasi Lemak (Coconut Rice)

When I was still living in Malaysia and in primary school, Nasi Lemak is what I had for recess every day. Traditionally these are packaged in banana leaf but at school it was plastic-lined newspaper. The school version took a very minimalist approach – rice, sambal, very few peanuts and ikan bilis and, if they were feeling generous, some cucumber. A couple of quarters of hard-boiled egg was a hit-the-jackpot kind of day. Recently I was lucky enough to delve into the secrets of Nasi Lemak specialist chef Shamil, who showed me how to steam the most aromatic nasi I've ever tasted in my life.

Rice

3 cups (600g) jasmine rice

10 pandan leaves, fresh or frozen*

1–2 stalks lemongrass, white part only, dry outer layers removed and discarded, bashed

1 red eschallot, peeled and halved

2 x 5mm slices ginger (skin on is fine), bashed

1½ teaspoons salt

2 teaspoons sugar

¾ cup (180ml) coconut cream

Bits and Pieces

¾ cup ikan bilis (dried anchovies)*

2 cups (500ml) vegetable oil

1 continental cucumber, halved lengthways, sliced into 5mm pieces

¾ cup (110g) salted beer nuts

4 hard-boiled eggs

1 portion Achar Penang (see page 212)

1 portion Sambal Lemak (see page 218)

banana leaves (optional)

Special Equipment: 25cm bamboo steamer OR vegetable steamer

Wash the rice then soak overnight in plenty of water. Drain for 10 minutes in a sieve.

Line a bamboo steamer OR steaming pot with pandan leaves. Sprinkle the lemongrass, eschallot and ginger over the pandan leaves and position steaming vessel over a wok or pot. Combine the rice with the salt, sugar and coconut cream and pour over the aromatics. Cover and steam for 15–30 minutes OR until the rice is tender. If you are using a bamboo steamer lid, place a piece of foil over the rice to help keep more steam in. An alternative to steaming is the normal absorption method. The grains won't be as nicely separated but you will get a more intense coconut flavour.

Preheat the oven to 180°C or 170°C fan-forced.

To fry the ikan bilis, heat the oil in a small saucepan over medium–high heat. To check if the oil is ready, drop in a few ikan bilis and if they turn golden in about 10 seconds, the oil is good to go. Fry all the ikan bilis at once until crispy and golden and scoop out with a slotted spoon, then transfer to a sieve lined with plenty of paper towel to drain. Set aside.

For an authentic Malaysian touch, line dinner plates with banana leaves basted with vegetable oil for gloss. Divide all the ingredients into individual portions or sharing plates to have at the centre of the table.

Nasi Lemak accompaniments are very much up to you. Instead of the Achar Penang, you could serve it with the Kunyit (Turmeric) Fried Chicken (see page 4) Prawn and Pineapple Curry (see page 76) or the Beef Rendang (see page 77). Try eating it with your hands ... it's more fun and tasty!

*Available from Asian grocers

Oodles of Noodles

Dark Hokkien Noodles

This is a dish my mum and Great Aunty Kim cook a lot for Sunday lunch or for big family get-togethers. There is always a big dish of this in the middle of the buffet table because the little ones love it. This is best eaten hot when the sauces haven't been completely soaked up by the noodles, giving them a delightfully slippery texture.

2 tablespoons vegetable oil

2 cloves garlic, peeled, finely chopped

250g pork neck/shoulder OR chicken, finely sliced

100g fish cake, sliced into 5mm thick pieces* (optional)

10 medium prawns, shelled, deveined and halved lengthways

½ medium cabbage, cut into 1cm slices OR equivalent amount of Chinese cabbage (wombok), choy sum OR bok choy, sliced into 4cm pieces

¼ cup (60ml) thick (caramel) soy sauce*

2 tablespoons oyster sauce

1 tablespoon light soy sauce

500g hokkien noodles

2 cups (500ml) chicken stock OR water

In a medium wok or large frypan heat the oil over high heat and sauté the garlic for a few seconds until slightly golden. Add the pork, fish cake and prawns and stir-fry until cooked through, then add the cabbage and stir-fry for a further 2 minutes. If using a finer Asian green like choy sum instead of cabbage, add at the end while the noodles are simmering so they are not overcooked and retain a nice crunch. Add the caramel soy, oyster sauce, light soy, noodles and chicken stock OR water. Simmer until cabbage and noodles are just tender and stock has reduced a little. Serve immediately portioned into individual bowls or on a large platter to share.

*Fish cakes and thick soy sauce are available from Asian grocers. Fish cakes are found in the fridge or freezer section. Thick soy is also called caramel soy but is different from kecap manis or dark soy.

Korean Sweet Potato Starch Noodles (Japchae)

My favourite comfort food is noodles. I can demolish mountains of the stuff. I love everything from a Vietnamese pho or a Malaysian laksa to a Thai pepper broth with glass vermicelli. This recipe uses Korean sweet potato noodles, a robust, translucent noodle with a fantastic springy texture.

300g Korean sweet potato starch
  noodles*
⅓ cup (80ml) sesame oil
3 cloves garlic, peeled, chopped
300g pork neck/shoulder, cut into
  matchsticks
12 medium (about 4cm diameter) dried
  shiitake mushrooms soaked in hot
  water for 20 minutes, water squeezed
  out and thinly sliced
⅓ cup (80ml) light soy sauce
¼ cup (60ml) oyster sauce
2 medium carrots coarsely grated
4–5 spring onions, green part only,
  sliced diagonally
1 bunch of coriander including stalks,
  roughly chopped
salt & white pepper

In a medium–large pot, boil the potato noodles in plenty of water until al dente – they should be cooked all the way through and have no grainy or hard centre but a nice bit of resistance when you bite into them. Refresh in cold water, then drain and toss in 1 tablespoon of the sesame oil. Set aside in a colander.

In a medium non-stick frypan or wok, heat remaining sesame oil over medium heat and sauté garlic for a few seconds until lightly coloured. Add the pork and mushrooms and stir-fry until pork is cooked through and slightly browned. Add the soy sauce, oyster sauce and carrot. Remove from the heat and toss until combined.

Transfer the noodles to a large mixing bowl, add the pork mixture, spring onions, coriander, salt and pepper, and toss well. Serve immediately portioned into individual bowls or on a large platter to share.

*Available from Asian grocers

Char Hoon is a classic Hokkien dish from my dad's side of the family. I will never be able to eat this without thinking of my late Grandma and Grandpa Yeow. It's a dish I can fiendishly inhale – it's so delicious, so reassuring, every problem in the world evaporates when a bowl of it is sitting in front of me.

12 dried shiitake mushrooms

100g dried rice vermicelli*, broken into 3cm pieces

500g prawns, shelled, deveined and diced into 1cm pieces, shells reserved for stock

4 L Neutral Chicken Stock (see page 216) OR store-bought Asian-style chicken stock

¼ cup (30g) cornflour

½ cup (125ml) water

3 tablespoons cooking oil

2 teaspoons garlic, peeled and finely chopped

200g dried wheat noodles (Meen Seen)*

3 bunches choy sum*, finely chopped

2 carrots, coarsely grated

1 kg firm tofu*, broken into small pieces

2 teaspoons salt, OR to taste

½ teaspoon sugar

½ teaspoon white pepper

Soak the shiitake mushrooms in hot water for about 30 minutes OR until soft, then chop roughly. Soak the vermicelli in cold water for about 15 minutes OR until soft.

To make the broth, add the prawn shells to the chicken stock in a medium–large pot and boil for 30 minutes. Pass the stock through a sieve to remove the prawn shells then return stock to the pot and set aside.

Mix the cornflour with the water in a small bowl and set aside.

In a medium non-stick frypan, heat the oil over medium heat and sauté the garlic until slightly coloured. Add the prawn meat and mushrooms and sauté for about 10 seconds, then transfer to the stock. Add both noodles, choy sum, carrot and tofu and bring to the boil. Stir through the cornflour mixture to thicken, bring back to the boil and add the salt, sugar and pepper. Taste and season further if required. Serve hot.

If you want a bit of spice, the sambal for the Tearaway Dumpling Soup (see page 219) is also very nice with this dish.

*Available from Asian grocers. Firm tofu is also found in most supermarkets. Choy sum is found in some supermarkets and greengrocers.

Law Meen

These next two noodle dishes are in what I call the 'food cuddles' genre – soft, slippery, gruelly contentment in a bowl. Funnily enough, I've only made these a few times myself because they are dishes I love to eat when I go home to visit my mum and Great Aunty Kim. I guess you always want to reserve the right to play the helpless child – even at age 39.

1 tablespoon cornflour

¼ cup (60ml) water

2 tablespoons vegetable oil

2 cloves garlic, peeled and finely chopped

300g boneless chicken thighs, diced into 1cm pieces

250g prawn meat, diced into 1cm pieces

150g fish cake OR fish tofu*, sliced into 3mm pieces

2 L Neutral Chicken Stock (see page 216) OR store-bought Asian-style chicken stock

500g hokkien noodles

2 eggs, lightly whisked

1 tablespoon fish sauce

¼ teaspoon white pepper

salt, to taste

1 bunch choy sum*, sliced in half

¼ cup (60ml) black Chinkiang vinegar*, to serve (optional)

Mix the cornflour with the water in a small bowl and set aside.

In a large heavy-based non-stick pot, heat the oil over medium heat and sauté the garlic until it begins to turn golden. Add the chicken, prawn meat and fish cake and stir-fry for about 2 minutes OR until the chicken is cooked through. Add the chicken stock and hokkien noodles, bring to the boil then stir in the eggs. Add the fish sauce, white pepper and cornflour mixture, stir well and boil for about 10 seconds until the soup is slightly thickened, then add salt to taste. Add the choy sum just before serving, stir and cover.

Serve hot in individual bowls with black Chinkiang vinegar on the table for guests to help themselves – about 1 teaspoon per serve OR to taste. Mix the vinegar into the soup just before eating. The vinegar is traditional but an acquired taste.

*Available at Asian grocers. Choy sum is also available at some supermarkets and greengrocers.

Punchy Pasta

Spaghetti Puttanesca

Feeds 4

In the '90s this was practically the only pasta I ate. I'm sure it had something to do with the name, which, in Italian, translates to 'whore's spaghetti'. At the time I was a repressed Mormon so it was a source of amusement whenever I ordered it. This truly is a dish with a colourful personality, feisty with the strong flavours of anchovy, capers, olives and chilli. I also love it because it's a very economical dish to make, using preserved ingredients I always have in the fridge. I like to add some lemon zest and juice at the end to freshen what can otherwise end up being an assault of salt!

6 small or 5 medium–large vine-ripened
    tomatoes
⅓ cup (80ml) extra virgin olive oil
4–5 anchovy fillets, roughly chopped
3 cloves garlic, peeled, finely sliced
1–2 tablespoons capers or halved
    caperberries
6–7 black olives, pitted and roughly
    chopped
1 teaspoon dried chilli flakes
5 L water
3 tablespoons cooking salt
500g spaghetti
1 teaspoon lemon zest
1 teaspoon lemon juice (optional)
¼ cup chopped flat-leaf parsley, plus
    extra for serving

To peel the tomatoes, remove the stems and score around the middle of each tomato. Place the tomatoes in a pot or bowl and submerge them completely in freshly boiled water then weigh them down with a small plate and allow to sit for 15 minutes. Drain and rinse with cold water before handling and the skins should slide off with ease. Roughly chop and set aside.

Heat the olive oil and the anchovy fillets in a medium non-stick frypan over medium heat until the anchovies have dissolved into the oil. Add the garlic, capers and olives and sauté for about 10 seconds until the garlic is fragrant but not coloured. Add the peeled tomatoes and chilli and simmer for 10 minutes OR until reduced and thickened. Turn off the heat and cover.

To cook the pasta, bring the water and salt to the boil in a large pot. As a rule it's usually 1 tablespoon of salt per litre of boiling water but the sauce in this dish is salty enough. Add the spaghetti and as soon as it slumps, push the exposed portion into the boiling water and stir immediately to prevent the pasta from sticking together. Agitate the pasta vigorously for about 10 seconds then boil for around 10 minutes OR until the pasta feels ever so slightly undercooked to the bite. Immediately fish out with tongs and toss into the sauce. Return the pan to high heat and cook for about 5 seconds more after it starts to bubble so the sauce thickens slightly. Remove from the heat and add the lemon zest and juice, and parsley then toss and garnish with more freshly chopped parsley before serving.

Al dente (to the tooth) pasta – time is of the essence if you want to achieve perfectly al dente pasta so don't worry about draining it. Fish the pasta out of the boiling water and drop it straight into the sauce. It took me ages to be convinced that the residual starchy water actually does help thicken the sauce and coat the pasta beautifully, making each bite superbly flavourful. You can also do away with the old trick of adding oil to the boiling water to prevent sticking – agitating the pasta at the beginning of the cooking process will do the job better. Oiling will also prevent the sauce from sticking to the pasta!

Prawn, Smoked Salmon & Squid Ink Fettuccine

I think it's safe to say that the Aussie version of Italian often lacks discipline whereas 'proper' Italian tends to thrive on very few but high-quality seasonal ingredients. However, I concede there's a time and place for everything and this came out of having to make something with what I had in the fridge one night. Whatever it lacks in subtlety, it makes up for by being really yummy.

¼ cup (60ml) olive oil

2 cloves garlic, peeled, finely chopped

2 medium brown onions, peeled, diced into 6mm cubes

30g unsalted butter

350g fresh prawn meat, diced into 1cm chunks

150g smoked salmon, cut into small pieces

¾ cup (100g) frozen baby peas

5–6 medium tomatoes, diced into 2cm chunks

¾ cup (180ml) white wine

⅓ cup crème fraiche OR cream

2 teaspoons finely chopped dill

½ cup finely chopped chives OR flat-leaf parsley

5 L water

5 tablespoons cooking salt

400g egg squid ink fettuccine or dry linguine

salt, to taste

freshly cracked pepper, to taste

zest of 1 lemon (optional)

¼ cup chopped flat-leaf parsley

To make the sauce, heat the olive oil, garlic and onion in a large non-stick frypan over medium heat. Sauté until the onions and garlic are translucent but not coloured. Remove from the heat and set aside.

In a second smaller non-stick frypan, heat the butter over high heat until it is foamy and golden brown. Add the prawns and salmon and sauté very briefly until the edges are slightly caramelised. Transfer to the large frypan, add the peas, tomato and white wine and simmer for about 10 seconds. Taste to check the wine is cooked out before adding the crème fraiche, dill and chives. Toss or stir, then turn heat off.

Bring the water and salt to the boil in a large pot and add the pasta. As soon as the fettuccine slumps, push the exposed portion into the boiling water and stir immediately to prevent the pasta from sticking together. Agitate the pasta vigorously for about 10 seconds then boil for around 10 minutes OR until the pasta feels ever so slightly undercooked to the bite. Immediately fish the pasta out with tongs, drop into the sauce and cook over high heat. Toss a few times before adding salt and a good amount of black pepper. Garnish with a small amount of lemon zest and parsley and serve immediately.

Sticky Rice

Glutinous Rice with Mango Sorbet & Salty Coconut Custard

This is my favourite Thai dessert and it's a great example of creating a huge amount of flavour with very few ingredients. Traditionally this is eaten with fresh mango, but if it isn't in season sorbet or purée made with frozen mangoes is a great substitute.

1 cup (200g) glutinous rice*
2 frozen mango cheeks, defrosted
100ml coconut milk
¾ teaspoon salt
¼ teaspoon pandan paste (pandan aroma pasta)*

Custard
½ cup (125ml) coconut cream
2 tablespoons caster sugar
¼ teaspoon salt

Special Equipment: ice-cream churner + blender + trivet

Soak the glutinous rice overnight in plenty of water then rinse in a sieve and drain for 10 minutes.

Blitz the mango cheeks in a blender until smooth, then pass through a sieve to catch and remove any fibres. Transfer the mango purée into an ice-cream churner and churn until stiff, then transfer to an airtight plastic container and freeze for about 3 hours OR until set. If you don't own an ice-cream machine simply chill the purée in the refrigerator.

Combine the rice, coconut milk and salt in a heatproof bowl or baking tin, mix and place on a trivet inside a large wok or pot with a lid, add enough water to reach the top of the trivet, cover and steam over high heat for about 40 minutes OR until the rice is cooked through. Watch the water level closely when the rice is steaming as it will evaporate very quickly – have a kettle of boiled water nearby so you can top up the water easily. Remove from the heat, drizzle the pandan paste over the rice and loosen the rice grains with a fork. Cover the bowl with a plate or cover loosely with cling wrap and allow to cool to room temperature.

To make the *custard*, combine the coconut cream, caster sugar and salt in a small saucepan and bring to the boil, stir, then remove from the heat and set aside to cool to room temperature.

To serve, divide the rice into 4 portions – break into chunks or press into a mould. Drizzle 2 tablespoons of coconut custard over each serve then top with mango ice-cream or purée and serve immediately.

> The glutinous rice should be eaten on the day it's made. Do not refrigerate it as it will go rock hard, but if you do it can be revived by steaming for 10 minutes over high heat.

*Available from Asian grocers

Rempah Udang

This is a classic Nyonya dish, an incredibly aromatic crumble of spicy, sweet, salty shrimp and coconut, stuffed into glutinous rice, wrapped in a banana leaf and grilled.

Sticky Rice

4 cups (800g) glutinous rice*, soaked overnight in plenty of water, rinsed, drained

400ml coconut milk

1½ teaspoons salt

Kerisik

1½ cups (90g) dried shredded coconut

Rempah

1 Spanish onion OR 4 red eschallots, peeled and roughly sliced

3 cloves garlic, peeled, sliced roughly

5 stalks lemongrass, white part only, dry outer layers removed, thinly sliced

3cm piece of galangal*, peeled (fattest part), thinly sliced

3cm piece of turmeric*, peeled and finely sliced or 1 tablespoon ground turmeric

15g belachan*, roughly chopped

10 small + 5 large dried red chillies*, deseeded, snipped into small pieces, soaked in ½ cup (125ml) boiling water for 30 minutes

3 tablespoons ground coriander

3 tablespoons caster sugar

½ teaspoon salt

⅓ cup (80ml) vegetable oil + extra for assembly

1 packed cup dried shrimp*, soaked in boiling water for 20 minutes, drained, finely chopped

⅓ cup (80ml) coconut cream

30 pieces banana leaf, cut into 15 x 15cm squares

vegetable oil, for brushing

60 toothpicks with sharp tips

Special Equipment: trivet for steaming + 24cm round cake tin + large wok with a domed lid OR a large metal Chinese steamer + blender + mini food processor

Combine the rice, coconut milk and salt in the cake tin, mix and place on a trivet inside a large wok. Fill with enough water to reach the top of the trivet, cover and steam over high heat for about 40 minutes OR until the rice is tender. The lid must be snug or the rice will not steam properly. Before the rice cools down, loosen the grains with a fork and set aside.

To make the kerisik, dry toast the coconut in a medium frypan over medium heat, tossing regularly until it is a deep golden brown. Transfer to a mortar and pestle or a mini food processor and grind into a grainy paste. Set aside.

To make the rempah, combine the onion, garlic, lemongrass, galangal, turmeric, belachan, chillies and chilli water in a blender and blend until it forms a smooth paste. Mix with the coriander, sugar and salt in a small bowl and set aside.

In a heavy-based non-stick saucepan or seasoned wok, heat the oil over medium heat, then sauté the chopped shrimp for 1 minute before adding the rempah. Cook for about 15 minutes OR until most of the liquid has evaporated and the mixture appears pulpy and is a deeper brown. Add the kerisik and coconut cream and cook, stirring continuously, until you have a moist crumble with no liquid. Set aside.

To prepare the banana leaves, fill a large saucepan with water and bring to the boil. Drop 3–4 banana leaves into the pan at a time and blanch for 10 seconds before refreshing in a large bowl of cold water (to retain the bright green colour and stop leaves from cooking further). Transfer the leaves to a colander to drain, then dry each piece with a clean tea towel.

To assemble the parcels, brush each piece of banana leaf generously with vegetable oil, place a tablespoonful of sticky rice onto the leaf in a flat rectangular shape, approximately 10 x 3cm in size. Spread 2 tablespoons of the rempah mixture on top then another layer of the rice. Fold one edge of the banana leaf over the rice, enclosing it in a cylinder. Gently squash to flatten the parcel a little before folding the sides in and securing with a toothpick on either side.

Eat the rempah udang as is or grill lightly to infuse the parcel with a lovely smoky flavour and fragrance from the banana leaf. Store in an airtight container and eat at room temperature on same day. To reheat, pile the parcels on top of one another and steam for 7–10 minutes over high heat. Good luck!

*Available from Asian grocers. For notes on dried chillies, see page 226.

Sophisticated Spuds

Potatoes with Garlic, Chilli & Spinach

I have been tremendously lucky to have travelled to many places and met so many wonderful food personalities in Australia, including the Simone family. They run Simone's in Bright, Victoria. This brilliant recipe, inspired by chef and owner Patrizia Simone is intended as a shared side but I often cook it for myself as a main meal when I'm dining solo. Warning: crazily moreish!

1kg potatoes, any kind, peeled and
   quartered

¼ cup (60ml) olive oil + more if you think
   the dish needs it

2 cloves garlic, peeled and sliced

1 teaspoon dried chilli flakes

1 large bunch of spinach OR silverbeet,
   stalks and leaves separated,
   leaves sliced into 5mm strips, stalks
   finely sliced

salt and pepper, to taste

1 lemon wedge

In a medium–large saucepan, cover the potatoes with water and bring to the boil. Drain and set aside.

In a large non-stick frypan, heat the olive oil, garlic and chilli over low–medium heat until the oil is fragrant but the garlic is not at all coloured. Add the spinach stalks and sauté for about 1 minute OR until tender, then add the leaves and cook until wilted and soft. Add the potatoes and salt, coarsely mashing into the spinach with an eggflip or spatula to keep some texture. Mix in the salt, pepper and a squeeze of lemon and serve hot with a little olive oil drizzled over the top. However, as a leftover snack, it's also delicious cold.

Hazelnut Potatoes

The combination of earthy mash with the crunch and oil of hazelnuts is truly heavenly. Serve as a side with any meat or fish dish.

¼ cup (35g) hazelnuts

1kg Dutch cream, Coliban or Desiree potatoes, peeled and quartered

70g unsalted butter, diced into 2cm cubes

1½ teaspoons salt, OR to taste

cracked black pepper

½ cup milk (125ml) + another ½ cup if potatoes made ahead of time

1 tablespoon hazelnut oil

Special Equipment: potato ricer, mouli OR use a fork and sieve

To dry toast the hazelnuts, heat them in a small frypan over medium heat, shaking the pan occasionally to make sure they are cooked evenly, but a few black spots is fine. The skins will start fizzing and cracking and when you can see most of the skins have come loose, remove from the heat. Transfer the nuts onto a clean tea towel and rub until the skins fall off – this must be done while they are hot. Ignore any stubborn skins that refuse to be removed as these won't spoil the dish. Roughly chop the nuts and set aside.

In a medium–large saucepan, cover the potatoes with water and bring to the boil. Drain and, while still hot, press through a potato ricer OR mouli OR use a fork and push through a sieve. Add the butter, salt, pepper and milk then whisk until smooth. Add more milk if you want a softer mash. Just before serving drizzle the hazelnut oil and sprinkle the chopped hazelnuts over the potato, then serve immediately.

George's Moussaka

The first time I tasted this George Calombaris recipe, I had it for dinner, breakfast the next morning, lunch and then for dinner again the next night, I loved it so much. If you've never had it before, it's layers of beautifully spiced ground meat cooked in tomato and baked with layers of silky, smoky, chargrilled eggplant. It's sure to become a family favourite.

2 large eggplants, cut lengthways into
    5mm slices
⅓ cup (80ml) olive oil + extra for grilling
    eggplant and greasing
2 medium–large capsicums
500g minced pork
500g minced lamb
1 teaspoon cumin seeds
1 teaspoon ground cinnamon
1 tablespoon dried oregano
2 cardamom pods

Sauce
2 onions, peeled, finely chopped
2 cloves garlic, peeled, finely chopped
800g tin crushed tomatoes
2 tablespoons fresh sage, finely
    chopped

Béchamel
3 cups (750ml) milk
1 onion, studded with 4 cloves and
    1 bay leaf
100g unsalted butter
½ cup (75g) plain flour
salt

120g kefalograviera (cheese) OR
    Parmesan cheese, coarsely grated

Special Equipment: 35 x 25cm lasagne dish

To prepare the eggplants, sprinkle each piece with salt and lay (slightly overlapping is fine) on wire racks for 30–40 minutes. Rinse under cold water to remove salt then pat dry with a clean tea towel.

Heat a small amount of the olive oil on a grooved skillet over high heat until smoking. Grill each piece of eggplant for about 30 seconds on each side or until both sides are barred with distinct char marks. Continue to oil the skillet as needed.

To prepare the capsicums, remove the core and stem, halve lengthways and press each piece down to flatten as much as possible. Lay, skin-side up, on baking trays lined with foil and grill on the highest shelf in your oven until the skins are blistered and black. The more burnt the skins are, the easier they will be to remove. Remove the tray from the oven, pull the sides of the foil to the centre and scrunch up to enclose the capsicums completely and leave for about 10 minutes, then peel and discard the skins. Chop the flesh finely and set aside.

To cook the mince, heat the remaining olive oil in a large non-stick frypan and sauté the pork and lamb over medium-high heat until the meat is brown. Add the cumin, cinnamon, oregano and cardamom, and cook, stirring continuously, for another 5 minutes. Season to taste and set aside.

To make the *sauce*, heat the remaining olive oil in a large non-stick saucepan over medium heat and sauté the onion and garlic until soft but not coloured. Add the tomato and capsicum and simmer for 15–20 minutes, stirring occasionally. Add the mince and sage and simmer, covered, for 15 minutes. Season to taste.

Preheat the oven to 180°C or 170°C fan-forced. To make the *béchamel*, combine the milk and prepared onion in a small saucepan and bring to a simmer over medium heat. In another medium non-stick saucepan melt the butter over medium heat. Add the flour and cook, stirring continuously, for 1 minute. Strain the milk, adding ¼ cup at a time into the butter and flour mixture, beating until smooth after each addition. If the sauce is not thick and pasty after the last addition of milk, cook further. Season with salt, mix and set aside.

Grease the lasagne dish with olive oil. Divide the eggplant pieces and mince into 3 portions and alternate layers beginning with a layer of eggplant. Spread the béchamel sauce evenly over the top and sprinkle with cheese. Bake for about 35 minutes until heated through and golden brown on top. Serve immediately.

Caponata & Ricotta Lasagne

This is a lovely, light, low-fat version of lasagne, using thinly sliced zucchini instead of pasta sheets. If you want the flavours to develop further, assemble and refrigerate overnight before baking. If you are vegetarian, omit the anchovies in the sauce.

1kg tomatoes

2 tablespoons olive oil

2 medium brown OR Spanish onions, peeled and chopped

2 cloves garlic, peeled, finely chopped

6 anchovy fillets (omit if vegetarian)

2 tablespoons capers

10 green olives, pitted and sliced

1 stick celery, diced into 1cm cubes

1 small–medium eggplant, diced into 1cm cubes

1 small red capsicum, diced into 1cm cubes

1 small yellow capsicum, diced into 1cm cubes

⅓ cup parsley including stalks, roughly chopped

salt & cracked black pepper

2–3 medium zucchinis, halved and cut lengthways into 3–4mm slices

600g low fat ricotta

⅔ cup (60g) Parmesan, finely grated

Special Equipment: 20 x 15cm lasagne dish with 5cm high sides OR something of similar proportions

To peel the tomatoes, remove the stem and score around the middle of each tomato. Place the tomatoes in a pot or bowl and submerge them completely in freshly boiled water then weigh down with a small plate and allow to sit for 15 minutes. Drain and rinse with cold water before handling and the skins should slide off with ease. Roughly chop and set aside.

Combine the olive oil, onions, garlic and anchovies in a medium saucepan over medium heat and cook until the onions are translucent and the anchovies are dissolved. Add the capers, olives, celery, eggplant and capsicums and cook until all the vegetables are tender. Add the tomatoes and cook until the mixture is nice and thick. Turn off the heat, stir in the parsley and add salt and pepper to taste. Set aside.

Preheat the oven to 180°C or 170°C fan-forced.

To prepare the zucchini, blanch for 10 seconds in boiling water. Drain in a colander and dry with paper towel. You can also grill the zucchini with some olive oil, which will infuse the dish with a lovely smokiness.

To assemble the lasagne, divide the caponata mixture, zucchini slices and ricotta in half and alternate layers starting with the caponata mixture. Finish with an even sprinkling of Parmesan. Bake for 20 minutes OR until heated through. If the Parmesan isn't a deep golden, grill the lasagne briefly. Divide into 4 portions and serve immediately.

Crunch

Banana Spring Rolls with Butterscotch Sauce

This reminds me very much of a Malaysian Goreng Pisang – a street snack of banana that's battered and deep-fried. Imagine the oozy sweetness of banana and butterscotch squelching from beneath layers of crispy skin shattering with every mouthful. I guarantee you will be feeling close to heaven.

5 largish bananas, peeled
1 heaped teaspoon plain flour
1 packet large spring roll wrappers*,
    20 x 20cm, thawed
1 tablespoon ground cinnamon
    (optional)
4 cups (1 L) vegetable oil
cream, to serve

Butterscotch Sauce
1 cup brown sugar
100g unsalted butter
½ cup (125ml) cream
generous pinch of salt

Special Equipment: Chinese spider

To make the *butterscotch sauce*, combine all the ingredients in a small saucepan and bring to the boil. Stir briefly to ensure the sugar is dissolved and set aside until required.

To prepare the bananas, cut each banana into 8 batons. In a small bowl, mix the flour with enough water to form a sticky paste.

To wrap, peel off one spring roll wrapper and lay it in front of you so a corner points north. Position 2 banana batons horizontally just under the centre line, then sprinkle a pinch of cinnamon over the top. Take the bottom corner of the wrapper and tuck it snugly over the banana batons. Fold both sides inwards to enclose the sides, then roll into a sausage, using the flour paste to secure the last corner of the skin in place. Repeat until all the bananas are used.

To fry, heat the oil in a medium–large pot over medium–high heat. To test if the oil is ready, immerse a pair of chopsticks in the oil so the tips touch the bottom of the saucepan and if a flurry of bubbles appears, the oil is ready. The best way to test is with a sacrificial spring roll. There is no danger of undercooking the filling but if you don't cook the spring rolls enough the inner layers won't crisp up completely. Cook in batches of 4 or 5 for about 30 seconds to 1 minute, turning so they colour evenly. Once they are a lovely golden brown all over, scoop up with a Chinese spider and lean them vertically in a colander lined with several layers of paper towel to drain. Serve with the butterscotch sauce and lashings of cream if you want additional happiness.

*Available from Asian grocers. Spring roll wrappers can also be found in some supermarkets.

Vegetarian Spring Rolls with Vietnamese Dipping Sauce

Makes about 20

It is a crying shame that this very scrumptious bit of finger food gets badly made all too often – carelessly wrapped parcels with exploded ends and fillings soggy with oil. It has a bad reputation from being a usual suspect in neglected food court bain maries, ready to be doused in radioactive-looking sweet and sour sauce. The truth is a well-made spring roll absolutely wins hearts at dinner parties and all you need is the humblest of ingredients. Success relies heavily on wrapping the parcels with patience and then frying them at the right temperature.

100g glass vermicelli noodles*
¼ cup (60ml) vegetable oil
2 cloves garlic, peeled and finely
    chopped
600g cabbage with thick stalks sliced
    away and discarded, leaves halved,
    sliced into 5mm strips
350g carrots, coarsely grated
2 tablespoons oyster sauce
2½ teaspoons light soy, OR to taste
¼ teaspoon white pepper
1 heaped teaspoon plain flour
1 packet large spring roll wrappers*,
    20 x 20cm, thawed
4 cups (1 L) vegetable oil

Dipping Sauce
1 clove garlic, peeled, finely chopped
⅓ cup (80ml) lemon juice
1 tablespoon fish sauce
2 tablespoons caster sugar
½–1 long red chilli, finely chopped

Special Equipment: Chinese spider

Soak the vermicelli in water for 15 minutes, then drain.

Combine the oil and garlic in a large non-stick frypan or wok and cook over medium–high heat until slightly coloured. Add the cabbage and carrot and stir-fry until the cabbage is only beginning to wilt. Add the vermicelli, oyster sauce, soy and white pepper and stir-fry for about 10 seconds or until the vermicelli is soft. Remove from the heat and spread out to cool completely on a large plate covered in 3 layers of paper towel. In a small bowl, mix the flour with enough water to form a sticky paste.

To wrap, peel off one spring roll wrapper and lay it in front of you so that a corner points north. Spread about 3 dessertspoons of filling mixture across the wrapper just under the centre line, leaving about 3cm of space either side. Take the bottom corner and tuck it snugly over the filling. Fold 3cm inwards to enclose the sides, then roll into a sausage, using the flour paste to secure the last corner of the wrapper in place. Repeat until all the filling is used.

To fry, heat the oil in a medium–large pot over medium–high heat. To test if the oil is ready, immerse a pair of chopsticks in the oil so the tips touch the bottom of the saucepan and if a flurry of bubbles appears, the oil is ready. The best way to test is with a sacrificial spring roll. There is no danger of undercooking the filling but if you don't cook the spring rolls enough the inner layers won't crisp up completely. Cook in batches of 4 or 5 for about 30 seconds to 1 minute, turning so they colour evenly. Once they are a lovely golden brown all over, scoop up with a Chinese spider and lean them vertically in a colander lined with several layers of paper towel to drain.

To make the *dipping sauce*, combine all the *dipping sauce* ingredients in a small bowl and mix until the sugar is dissolved. Serve the spring rolls hot or at room temperature.

If you are determined to be a carnivore, add 200g of pork or chicken mince to the stir-fry after sautéing the garlic and cook until the meat is cooked through before continuing to follow the recipe.

*Available from Asian grocers. Spring roll wrappers can also be found in some supermarkets.

Tasty Tofu

Steamed Soft Tofu with Brown Beans & Ginger

Feeds 1–2

This is a lovely dish I grew up eating with my Great Aunty Kim whenever she was on a special Buddhist diet during certain times in the lunar calendar. It uses very few ingredients, reflecting a minimalist style of eating that is meant to encourage reverence and reflection.

1 tablespoon finely shredded ginger

1 tablespoon vegetable or ricebran oil

300g silken or soft tofu*

1½–2 tablespoons brown beans*, rinsed, drained, roughly chopped

1 teaspoon soy sauce

generous pinch of caster sugar

⅓ long red chilli, seeds removed, finely sliced

Special Equipment: vegetable steamer

Combine the ginger and oil in a small saucepan and cook over medium heat. As soon as the ginger turns golden remove the saucepan from the heat and set aside.

Place the tofu in a rice bowl. Mix the brown beans, soy sauce and sugar in a separate bowl and pour over the tofu. Steam with the bowl sitting on a trivet in a covered pot OR place the bowl in the basket of a vegetable steamer for 5–7 minutes OR cover and microwave for 2 minutes. Pour the ginger oil and crispy ginger over the top, garnish with fresh chilli and serve with steamed jasmine rice as a shared or solo dish.

> Brown beans are usually packaged in a glass jar but most commonly come in two forms: whole beans in a runny sauce or brown bean paste in which the beans are blended into the sauce. Whole beans are best because the flavour is better and you can rinse them in a sieve under cold water and drain to remove some of the salt content.

*Available from Asian grocers. Silken and soft tofu is also available in the refrigerated section of most supermarkets.

Stir-fried Firm Tofu with Soy Beans & Pickled Cabbage

This is a dish inspired by a local sliver-in-the-wall Chinese joint in Adelaide that my friends and I have been going to since we were all at uni. It's a simple vegetarian stir-fry that's so delicious even the meat lovers never complain.

70g tinned Chinese pickled cabbage (sheet choy)*

3 tablespoons vegetable oil

2–3 cloves garlic, peeled, finely chopped

1 large chilli, finely sliced

180g frozen soy beans*, rinsed and drained

200g firm tofu*, cut into 5mm batons

1 tablespoon fish sauce OR light soy sauce (for vego)

1 tablespoon shaoxing rice wine*

¼ teaspoon caster sugar

Pour the pickled cabbage into a sieve, rinse well, then drain and set aside.

Combine the vegetable oil, garlic and chilli in a wok or large non-stick frypan and cook over high heat until the garlic turns a pale golden. Add the soy beans and pickled cabbage and toss for 10 seconds. Add the tofu, fish sauce, shaoxing and sugar, toss for a few more seconds and serve immediately with steamed jasmine rice.

*All available from Asian grocers. Shaoxing rice wine is also found in some supermarkets and firm tofu in most supermarkets.

Vego

This is a wonderful Buddhist vegetarian dish that I have often requested from my Great Aunty Kim since I was knee-high. I must have eaten mountains of the stuff by now but I still never tire of it. Please don't be put off by the sound of fermented bean curd – married with the wild array of fungi in this dish, it's absolutely delicious.

Mock Meat

3⅓ cups (500g) plain or 00 flour

1 cup (250ml) water

2 cups (500ml) vegetable oil

5–6 dried soy bean sticks*, snapped in half

Mushroom Stew

35g dried shiitake mushrooms, stems removed

15g cloud ear or black fungus mushrooms*

115g tigerlily buds* (Gum Chum or golden needles), woody tips cut off

7g black moss* (fat choy or hair vegetable)

¼ cup (60ml) vegetable oil

3–4cm piece of ginger, peeled and finely shredded

90g white fermented chilli bean curd* (Bak Fu Yee)

8 leaves Chinese cabbage (wombok)

350g mixed fresh mushrooms (3–4 types)

150g tinned champignons

100g tinned straw mushrooms*

½ cup (125ml) water

salt, to taste

50g glass vermicelli noodles*

light soy sauce, to taste

1 teaspoon sugar

Special Equipment: Chinese spider

To make the *mock meat*, combine the flour and water then knead for about 5 minutes until it is a smooth pliable dough. Cover with cling wrap and rest for 30 minutes.

Soak the shiitake mushrooms in hot water for about 30 minutes OR until completely soft, drain and squeeze excess moisture out. Soak the cloud ear in water for about 30 minutes OR until soft and expanded. Remove and discard woody parts, then drain. Soak the vermicelli in water for about 20 minutes, then drain. Soak the tigerlily buds in hot water for 15 minutes, rinse and squeeze excess moisture out. Soak the black moss in water for about 10 minutes, then drain.

Fill a large mixing bowl with water and place it in the sink. Remove the cling wrap, transfer the dough into a colander and immerse in the mixing bowl of water. Massage and knead the dough under the water, changing the water when it becomes very cloudy. Continue to massage the dough until the water is relatively clear and you have a rather unattractive lump of gluten – greyish, pitted and very elastic.

Roll and stretch the gluten into a long cylinder roughly 2cm in diameter, then snip with scissors into 2cm pieces. Rest the pieces on a plate and pat dry to prevent excessive spitting when frying. To fry the gluten, heat the oil in a medium saucepan over medium–high heat. To test if the oil is ready, drop a piece of gluten in (stand back when the gluten is lowered into the oil) and if it turns golden in about 10 seconds it's perfect but if it goes brown within 5 seconds, it's too hot. Fry in batches of 5 or 6 until puffed out and golden. Scoop out using a Chinese spider, drain on paper towel and set aside. Fry the soy bean sticks using the same method as the gluten.

Combine ¼ cup oil and ginger in a large heavy-based saucepan over medium heat and sauté the ginger until golden. Add the fermented bean curd and sauté for a few seconds then add the fried gluten, soybean sticks and the remaining ingredients except the black moss, vermicelli, soy sauce and sugar. Cover and simmer for 20 minutes. Add the black moss and vermicelli, mix and simmer for another 2 minutes. Add the sugar and season with soy sauce. Serve hot with steamed jasmine rice.

I always suggest using a Chinese spider when frying because you can collect a large number of fried items in one swift swoop, which avoids the odd item getting too much colour or burnt.

*Available from Asian grocers

Konnyaku Bundles with Wakame, Tofu & Chrysanthemum Greens

Konnyaku, also known as shirataki, is a Japanese-style noodle that contains a minuscule amount of carbohydrates. It is made from elephant or konjac yam and has no flavour of its own but does impart a delightfully weird crunch – quite un-noodle like. It is mostly water and glucomannan, a water-soluble dietary fibre, so it's a useful ingredient to have in the pantry if you are on a low-carb diet. I love this particular recipe because I always finish the meal feeling cleansed and restored.

200g chrysanthemum greens (Tung Ho)*

2 cups (500ml) Neutral Chicken Stock
   (see page 216)

15g wakame* (Japanese dried seaweed),
   broken into 4–5cm shards

300g soft or silken tofu*, diced into
   3cm cubes

1 tablespoon fish sauce, OR to taste

350g konnyaku noodles, rinsed and
   drained

pinch of white pepper

Wash the chrysanthemum greens, slice the ends off and cut into 5cm pieces including stalks.

Combine the chicken stock, wakame, tofu, fish sauce, konnyaku and white pepper in a medium saucepan and bring to the boil. Reduce the heat, add the chrysanthemum greens and simmer for about 5 seconds OR until the greens are blanched.

To serve, divide the konnyaku noodles into 2 bowls and scoop the hot broth over the top making sure the ingredients are evenly distributed.

> If you think you might struggle without meat, add 200g of fishballs or a firm-fleshed fish, cut into 3cm pieces, to the broth as it comes to the boil. For some spice you could also add a bit of kimchi to the soup (see page 8).

*Available from Asian grocers. Soft or silken tofu is also available in the refrigerated section of most supermarkets.

Sponge

Mama's Rice Bowl Steamed Sponge

Among a myriad of Nyonya specialties, my Grandma Yeow would always have this Chinese cake ready if she knew we were visiting. Traditionally, the size of the cake is determined by the size of the bowl you use to measure the ingredients – the same rice bowl is filled to the rim with eggs, then the same amount of sugar and flour. The trick is to get the lining of the baking paper right, otherwise your cake will end up a disfigured specimen in the water bubbling beneath. The texture is interesting – a cross between marshmallow and bread, with the flavour of custard. A perfect fat-free tea cake.

4 large (60g) free-range eggs

1 cup (230g) caster sugar

1 teaspoon natural vanilla extract OR pandan paste* (pandan aroma pasta)

1 cup (150g) plain flour, sifted

1½ teaspoons baking powder, sifted

*Available from Asian grocers

Special Equipment: 20cm bamboo steaming basket + large pot which fits the bamboo basket comfortably and is at least 3 times its height + lid + trivet with 5cm legs + funnel + electric cake mixer

To line a bamboo steaming basket well requires an old-fashioned trick my mum learnt in home economics as a girl. Firstly turn the bamboo basket upside down and trace around the edge on baking paper. Cut a little inside the tracing line so the circle will sit perfectly on the bottom of the basket without crinkling the edges. Secondly, wind a piece of baking paper around the circumference of the basket with a 5cm overlap. Trim it so the height is twice that of the bamboo basket and then place in front of you so the length of it runs horizontally. Take the bottom edge and fold a pleat, 1.5cm wide, upwards all along it. With a pair of scissors, snip from the edge up to the fold at 1cm intervals so you end up with something that looks like a fringe. Sit this piece of baking paper inside the bamboo steamer, with the fringe splayed out flat on the bottom of the steamer, and the fold wedged nicely into the corner of the basket. Place the circle over the top and you have a nice seal for the batter to be poured into. This method of lining can be used for any cake tin.

To prepare for steaming, place a steaming trivet at the bottom of the large pot. Pour enough water to reach halfway up the legs of the trivet. Bring water to the boil, then cover and turn the heat off.

To make the batter, combine the eggs, sugar and vanilla OR pandan paste in a large mixing bowl and beat with an electric mixer until mixture is pale, fluffy and triple its original volume. Very gently fold in the flour and baking powder. Pour the mixture into the lined bamboo steamer, then lower this carefully onto the trivet sitting in the pot of boiled water. Remember to use gloves – it's easy to forget steam burns! I prefer dishwashing gloves in this instance because they give you a bit more dexterity than a thick, cumbersome mitt. Reduce to a medium heat, cover and steam for about 20–30 minutes OR until an inserted skewer comes out clean.

Watch the water level closely. I have forgotten many times and had smoked sponge instead, which isn't quite the same, nor edible! To remedy a fast evaporating water level, VERY carefully pour boiled water into a funnel guided into the gap between the bamboo basket and pot. The funnel is to prevent you from splashing water all over the cake, which I have also done! Droplets of water will condense on the lid of the pot and fall onto your cake while it is cooking, but don't fret, your cake will be fine. Serve warm with coffee or tea.

Mum's Jam Roll

The smell of a freshly baked Swiss roll and warm strawberry jam is something that instantly makes me feel about five again. With my best friend Sarah's strawberry jam recipe, the entire roll is usually inhaled before it even has a chance to cool down.

Sarah's Strawberry Jam
Makes about 450ml (there will be spare for toast)
500g fresh or frozen strawberries
1 cup (250ml) water
300g sugar
2 tablespoons lemon juice

Swiss Roll
4 extra large eggs
½ cup (115g) caster sugar
1 teaspoon vanilla bean paste OR natural vanilla extract
2 tablespoons warm water
¾ cup (110g) plain flour
¼ cup wheaten cornflour
1¼ teaspoons baking powder
1 tablespoon vegetable oil

*For notes on sterilising glass jars, see page 219

Special Equipment: 32 x 22cm baking tray with 2cm high sides + electric cake mixer

To make the *jam*, combine the strawberries and water in a medium saucepan and bring to the boil. Boil for 10 minutes OR until the fruit is soft and plump. Add the sugar and lemon juice and continue to boil gently for a further 10 minutes OR until the 'wrinkle test' is positive. To do a wrinkle test, place a small plate in the freezer for a few minutes. Dollop a small spoonful on the cold plate and drag your finger through the jam – if the surface wrinkles up it's ready. If not, return to the boil and repeat the test every few minutes. Be careful at this stage, it's better that your jam be slightly under-gelled and full of fruitiness than being overpowered by the flavour of caramelised sugar. Immediately pour into sterilised glass jars*, seal, and keep jars inverted until completely cooled. For the jam roll, your jam may be warm or cooled.

Preheat the oven to 180°C or 170°C fan-forced.

To make a *Swiss roll*, combine the eggs, sugar and vanilla in a large mixing bowl and beat with an electric cake mixer until pale, fluffy and triple its original volume. Add the water and beat very briefly until just combined. Sift the flour, cornflour and baking powder directly into the egg mixture and fold gently in 3 batches with a silicone spatula. When folding, make sure you dig deep to ensure there are no pockets of flour sitting at the bottom of the mixing bowl. Trickle the oil into the batter and fold to combine. Pour into the baking tray lined with baking paper including up the sides and roll mixture around to fill the tray rather than spreading with a spatula. Just before baking, drop the tray from a 10cm height onto the benchtop to be rid of any large air bubbles. Bake for about 10–15 minutes OR until golden brown.

To roll a Swiss roll successfully you must work quickly to avoid cracking. As soon as you pull it out of the oven, plant the sponge sheet face down onto a tea towel generously dusted with icing sugar. Peel the baking paper away and be ready to slather on 1 cup of jam as if your life depended on it. Using the tea towel as leverage, roll the sponge sheet as snugly but as gently as possible with the longest side being the length of the jam roll. Use the tea towel to transfer the roll to a platter, trim to neaten the ends and serve – there's nothing like eating a huge slice of this warm!

• Because this jam roll is free of preservatives, you'll find it goes stale very quickly. To give it a second life, slice it into thin pieces and toast in the oven set at 100°C or 90°C fan-forced until crispy – perfect to dunk into coffee.
• Try filling the Swiss roll with Kaya (page 20), Blood Orange and Passionfruit Curd (page 21), Satsuma Plum Jam (page 164) or Banana Jam (page 165).

Satouma
Plum Jam

Jam

Satsuma Plum Jam

I didn't know I liked plum jam until my friend Sarah made some from an overflowing crop of Satsuma plums growing at a mutual friend's house. Now it's one of my favourites but our friend has since moved and the abundance of Satsuma jam is sorely missed by all of us. The trick to jam is to never overcook it because once you do, any subtle flavour from the fruit will be drowned out by the sickly sweet combination of over-caramelised fruit and sugar, and you're left with a generic-tasting jam made from an unidentifiable fruit.

500g Satsuma OR blood plums, halved
    and stones discarded
1 cup (250ml) water
300g white sugar
2 tablespoons lemon juice

To make the jam, combine the plums and water in a medium saucepan and bring to the boil. Boil for 10 minutes OR until the fruit is soft and plump. Add the sugar and lemon juice and continue to boil gently for a further 10 minutes OR until the 'wrinkle test' is positive. To conduct a wrinkle test – place a small plate in the freezer for a few minutes and when the jam is getting close to setting point, dollop a small spoonful on the cold plate. Drag your finger through the jam and if the surface wrinkles up, it's ready. If this is not the case, return to the boil and repeat the test every few minutes. At this stage, be careful not to overcook the jam. It's better that your jam be slightly under-gelled and the flavour of the fruit be retained.

When the jam is ready, immediately pour into sterilised glass jars*, seal and then keep jars inverted for about 2 hours OR until completely cooled. Unopened jams can last for years but using them within a year is recommended.

*For notes on sterilising glass jars, see page 219

Banana, Lime & Cinnamon Jam

This recipe was born out of curiosity. As I stared at a bunch of spotty bananas in my fruit bowl, I wondered, has anyone ever made banana jam? The answer – Yes! I pastiched several recipes together and arrived at this – delicious on pancakes, scones and toast, especially when paired with peanut butter and honey.

3½ cups diced very ripe bananas
¼ cup (60ml) freshly squeezed lime juice
1 cup (230g) caster sugar
½ cup (125ml) water
1 teaspoon ground cinnamon

In a medium mixing bowl, toss the bananas in the lime juice. In a small saucepan, bring the sugar and water to the boil, stirring until the sugar is dissolved. Add the bananas, lime juice and cinnamon and cook over low–medium heat for about 15 minutes OR until the mixture thickens to a consistency you desire. Stir every few minutes with a wooden spoon to prevent the sides and bottom from catching and mash with a potato masher throughout the cooking process to break down the larger chunks. Immediately transfer to sterilised glass jars* and invert until completely cooled. Keep in the fridge for up to 3 months.

*For notes on sterilising glass jars, see page 219

Azuki (Red) Bean & Coconut Icy Poles

This dessert was inspired by an icy pole we occasionally bought from a door-to-door hawker when I was still a child living in Malaysia. I vividly remember that whenever we heard him ring his bicycle bell, our cook Lin Cheh Cheh (I called her big sister Lin) and my Great Aunty Kim would yell to each other and clamber to find coins. This is also a favourite of my dad's.

Azuki Beans
⅓ cup azuki (red) beans*
pinch of salt

Coconut Custard
⅔ cup (160ml) coconut milk
3 tablespoons caster sugar
generous pinch of salt
1 pandan leaf*, shredded by hand
    lengthways and tied into a knot
    (optional)

Special Equipment: food processor OR mortar and pestle + 4 icy-pole moulds that hold about 80ml each

Soak the *azuki beans* overnight in plenty of water, then drain.

To cook the azuki beans, boil them in plenty of water with the salt for 1 hour OR until the beans are very soft and can be easily mashed between your fingers. Have a kettle of boiled water nearby to top the water up whenever necessary. Drain and reserve 2 tablespoons of the cooking water. Blitz the beans with the reserved cooking water in a mini food processor or mash with a mortar and pestle until you have a fine paste. You may pass the mixture through a sieve if you want a smoother finish, but I like some texture in the beans.

To make the *coconut custard*, combine all the ingredients in a small pot and bring to the boil. Give the pandan leaf a good stab to encourage infusion. Cover with a lid and allow to cool to room temperature.

To make the icy poles, dollop in enough azuki bean paste to fill the moulds halfway. Freeze for 1 hour, then fill to 5mm short of the rim with the cooled coconut custard. Freeze for 30 minutes before positioning ice-cream sticks into the icy poles, then freeze for another 2 hours. If you are having trouble getting the icy poles to dislodge from the moulds, run them under warm water.

*Available from Asian grocers. Pandan leaves are found fresh and in the freezer section at Asian grocers.

Azuki (Red) Bean Hedgehog Buns

I first saw these gorgeous little buns being made at a food festival about four years ago. I was utterly mesmerised as Chef Yu Bo from Chengdu, China, and his wife, Dai Shuang, demonstrated this dish – with exactly 120 snips for 120 quills per hedgehog. If dexterity is not your strength, you can make a conventional round bun and with the blunt end of a skewer place a dot of red food colouring at the centre – this is the Chinese way, so good luck follows you even through to your steamed buns!

Azuki Bean Paste

⅔ cup azuki (red) beans*

pinch of salt

½ cup (115g) caster sugar

1 portion of Flower Buns dough –
    follow until the end of 1st prove
    (see page 17)

1 teaspoon black sesame seeds

*Available from Asian grocers

Special Equipment: food processor OR mortar and pestle + sharp pair of tweezers + sharp manicure scissors + large 25cm bamboo steamer with lid

Soak the azuki beans overnight in plenty of water and drain.

To cook the beans, boil them in plenty of water and a pinch of salt for 1 hour OR until the beans are very soft and can be easily mashed between your fingers. Have a kettle of boiled water nearby to top the water up whenever necessary. Drain, but reserve 2 tablespoons of the cooking water. Blitz the beans with the reserved cooking water in a mini food processor or mash with a mortar and pestle until you have a fine paste. You may pass the mixture through a sieve if you want a smoother finish, but I like some texture in the beans.

Transfer the beans to a small non-stick saucepan, add the sugar and cook, stirring continuously, over medium heat until most of the water content has evaporated and you have a thick paste. Set aside to cool.

To make a hedgehog, tear off a golfball-sized chunk of dough (about 40g), shape it into a ball, squash with the palm of your hand, then, using your fingers, ease the circle into a 5mm thick teardrop shape. Place a teaspoonful of *azuki bean paste* at the round end of the tear, then gather the sides in and begin pinching into a ball but then follow the pinching to the pointy end to form a tear drop shape. Sit it with the seam facing down, then with a very sharp pair of tweezers, position the eyes and nose at the pointy end with 3 sesame seeds and push in lightly to make sure the seeds are secure.

To create the quills use the sharp tip of some manicure scissors to snip partially into the dough (be careful not to pierce through to azuki red bean filling) in arcs that begin around the face, then work gradually towards its bottom. Repeat with the remaining dough and filling until you have about 20 hedgehogs. Rest each hedgehog on a small square of baking paper and allow to prove for 30–40 minutes OR until doubled in size then place in a large 25cm bamboo steamer, cover and steam for 5–6 minutes over high heat. Serve immediately.

These will keep in an airtight container in the freezer for up to 2 months or in the fridge for 2 weeks, so you can make them ahead of time for dinner parties and revive them with a 5-minute steam.

Whip It!

Mini Coffee & Almond Pavlovas

To be honest, pavs aren't my strong point but when I make them they're still demolished in the blink of an eye! This recipe is inspired by Christine of Port Lincoln, South Australia, mother of oyster farmer Lester Marshall – the rascal who fed me the five-year-old 100 gram mollusc! He had told me about his mum's legendary pavs, which were usually only made for special occasions and the visit from *Poh's Kitchen* was considered worthy, so we were in for a treat. No matter how many fancy desserts I eat, it's always the simple old-fashioned ones that leave a lasting impression.

4 extra large egg whites (about 140g)
pinch of salt
1 cup (230g) caster sugar
2 teaspoons instant espresso coffee
    granules
2 teaspoons wheaten cornflour
1 teaspoon white or red vinegar
1 cup (155g) almonds
2 portions of Crème Chantilly
    (see page 214)

Special Equipment: electric cake mixer + mortar and pestle

Preheat the oven to 140°C or 130°C fan-forced.

To make the meringue, whisk the egg whites and salt with an electric cake mixer until soft peaks form. Add the sugar, 1 tablespoon at a time, and whisk after adding each spoonful for about 7–10 seconds. Crush the espresso coffee granules to a powder using a mortar and pestle, combine with the cornflour and sift both directly into the meringue. Add the vinegar, then fold until combined.

Dollop even amounts of mixture onto a large baking tray lined with baking paper, leaving about 3cm between each one. This quantity will make 6–8 mini pavlovas. If you want to be more precise draw 9cm diameter circles on the baking paper as a guide. Using a spoon, shape the pavlovas into fat discs 2–3cm high. Bake for 1 hour, then turn the heat off and cool completely in the oven before using (overnight is best).

To roast the almonds, preheat the oven to 170°C or 160°C fan-forced. Spread the almonds on a baking tray and roast for 7–10 minutes, then chop roughly. I'm not usually a fan of the microwave, but to speed things up, you can heat the almonds for 2 minutes on the highest setting instead.

To assemble, arrange the mini pavlovas on a serving platter, slather the desired amount of Créme Chantilly on top and then sprinkle with the chopped almonds.

When working with egg whites, always ensure the whisk and bowl are utterly clean and dry. Also, make sure there is not a trace of egg yolk to be found as the fat content will prevent the egg whites from fluffing up into stiff peaks and instead they will remain a limp watery mess. Egg whites freeze very well, so don't throw them away, portion them into small snap-lock bags for easy handling at a later date.

Marshmallow Pavlova Roulade with Strawberry, Balsamic, Basil & Vanilla

It's a big call but this is seriously one of the most memorable desserts I've ever tasted in my life. It's inspired by a really clever Karen Martini recipe I saw years ago. First, there's the soft marshmallowy pavlova (and who doesn't love a pav? It's un-Australian surely?), luscious mascarpone made lighter with the sharpness of yoghurt, then that exquisite Italian combination of strawberries, vanilla and aged balsamic. Throw in a few leaves of shredded mint and basil and you've added an intriguing savoury note. Love, love, love.

Meringue

5 large egg whites (about 175g)
pinch of salt
½ cup (115g) caster sugar
1 teaspoon natural vanilla extract
1 tablespoon wheaten cornflour
½–¾ cup (45–65g) flaked almonds

Filling

200g mascarpone
200g natural unsweetened yoghurt
1 vanilla bean, split, seeds scraped out
    or 1 teaspoon vanilla bean paste
2 tablespoons icing sugar

Topping

375g strawberries, tops discarded,
    each sliced lengthways into 6 pieces
3 tablespoons aged balsamic
2 tablespoons caster sugar
6 large basil leaves, finely sliced
7 mint leaves, torn

Special Equipment: electric cake mixer + 35 x 26cm baking tray OR at least similar proportions

Preheat the oven to 180°C or 170°C fan-forced. Line a baking tray with baking paper including the sides. Set aside.

To make the *meringue*, whisk the egg whites and a pinch of salt with an electric cake mixer until soft peaks form. Add the sugar, 1 tablespoon at a time, whisking after adding each spoonful for about 7–10 seconds. Add the vanilla and sift the cornflour over the meringue, then fold until combined. Spread the meringue carefully over the baking tray then sprinkle evenly with the almonds. Flatten any that are upright to avoid burning. Turn the oven down to 150°C or 140°C fan-forced and bake for 25 minutes. To test, give the surface of the pav a gentle prod to see if there is a bit of resistance. If yes, it's ready.

Remove the pavlova from the oven and immediately place it face down onto a tea towel dusted with icing sugar. While it's warm and with the baking paper still attached, use the tea towel as leverage to roll the pavlova up with the longest part of the rectangle being the length of the roulade. Allow to cool completely.

To prepare the *filling*, whisk the filling ingredients in a medium mixing bowl to combine and set aside.

To prepare the *topping*, combine all the topping ingredients in a medium mixing bowl and leave to macerate for 5 minutes before serving.

When the pavlova sheet is completely cooled, carefully uncoil it just enough to remove the baking paper. Slather the filling into the cavity and roll up again. Carefully transfer the filled roulade onto a rectangular platter. If you aren't ready to serve, chill the roulade and only pour the topping over at the very last minute.

Always save scraped vanilla pods for stuffing into your sugar jar – vanilla sugar!

Good Pud

This is a lovely rendition of an old favourite – I love this version because using croissants makes for a much lighter pudding and no need to butter the bread. There's nothing more comforting to end an autumn or winter meal with.

butter, for greasing

3 large (200g) butter croissants, sliced into 3 layers then torn into thirds

1½ cups fresh or frozen raspberries

2 tablespoons dried currants

⅓ cup (45g) slivered almonds, lightly toasted

icing or caster sugar, for dusting

Frangelico, to serve (optional)

Custard

60g caster sugar

1 teaspoon vanilla bean paste or seeds scraped from 1 vanilla bean

3 large eggs

200ml cream

200ml milk

Special Equipment: 20cm round ceramic dish, 5cm high sides OR something that holds a similar volume (shape is not an issue)

Preheat the oven to 180°C or 170°C fan-forced.

To make the *custard*, whisk the caster sugar, vanilla, eggs, cream and milk briefly in a medium mixing bowl to combine.

To prepare the pudding, grease the ceramic dish with the butter, then sprinkle half the raspberries, half the currants and one-third of the almonds evenly over the bottom of the dish. Soak half the croissants in the custard mixture for 10–20 seconds before arranging over the fruit and almonds. Pour about ½ cup of the custard mixture over the croissants before creating another layer with the remaining berries, currants and one-third of the almonds. Soak the remaining croissants in the custard and arrange the final layer, top with the remaining custard mixture, pressing gently to encourage croissants to soak in more custard, then cover with a generous dusting of icing or caster sugar and remaining almonds. Bake for 30–45 minutes OR until the top has formed a golden crust. Serve immediately with pouring cream or lightly whisked Crème Chantilly (see page 214) and a cheeky dash of Frangelico.

Sour Cherry Clafoutis

This is a recipe I've been making since my mid-twenties. It's so simple that even the most amateur cook will be able to achieve a brilliant result. To anyone out there hoping to impress a romantic prospect, this dessert is your wingman! No delicate creaming or folding required. Bar macerating the cherries in liquor, and deliberately having to burn some butter, it's an unceremonious affair of dumping all the ingredients in a bowl, mixing, pouring and baking. I promise you, nothing can go wrong or my name is Frank!

500g drained Morello cherries

2 tablespoons caster sugar

2 tablespoons Frangelico OR kirsch

10g unsalted butter, melted, for greasing

¼ cup (55g) caster sugar + ⅓ cup (80g)
    for sprinkling

Batter

80g unsalted butter

⅔ cup (100g) plain flour, sifted

pinch of salt

3–4 large eggs

½ cup (115g) caster sugar + extra for
    crust

zest of 1 lemon OR orange

1 teaspoon natural vanilla extract

150ml milk

150ml cream

Special Equipment: 30 x 22cm oval baking dish with 4–5cm high sides OR any dish that holds a similar volume (shape is not an issue)

Preheat the oven to 180°C or 170°C fan-forced.

Combine the cherries, sugar and liqueur of choice in a small bowl and allow to macerate for 10 minutes.

Using a pastry brush, grease the baking dish with butter, brushing all the way up the sides and taking care not to miss any spots. Spoon the caster sugar into the dish and shake so granules thoroughly coat the butter. Set aside.

To make the *batter*, melt the butter in a small saucepan over medium–high heat until the butter turns brown. Remove from the heat and set aside.

In a medium mixing bowl, combine the remaining batter ingredients and whisk until smooth. Add the burnt butter, cherries and any resulting syrup, then stir with a wooden spoon and tip the mixture into the prepared baking dish. Sprinkle caster sugar evenly over the surface of the batter and bake for 30–35 minutes OR until the top of the clafoutis forms a lovely golden crust. Serve with hot Crème Chantilly (see page 214).

Easy Peasy

Lemonade Scones

These are *the* easiest, most fail-safe scones in the world. You can achieve miraculously light ones without having baked a single scone in your life. Simply stir, pat, cut and bake – scone demystified. To be ever ready for that sudden scone-attack, it's useful to keep a can of lemonade in the pantry.

3 cups (450g) plain flour, plus extra for
   dusting
4½ teaspoons baking powder
½ teaspoon salt
1 cup (250ml) cream
1 cup (250ml) lemonade
butter, for greasing
2–3 tablespoons milk

Special Equipment: 6–8cm scone/pastry cutter

Preheat the oven to 200°C or 190°C fan-forced.

Combine the flour, baking powder and salt in a medium mixing bowl. Whisk briefly to combine, make a well in the centre, then add the cream and lemonade. With a spatula, using a circular motion, slowly gather the flour into the centre until you have a sticky mass that is just combined. Tip the dough onto a clean, well-floured benchtop. Sift more flour over the top of the dough before patting it down to a thickness of 3cm and cut with a scone/pastry cutter, flouring the cutter in between scones, OR you can simply cut the slab into a grid and make square ones.

Grease a baking sheet/tray with butter and arrange the scones so they are butted up against one another (for support as they rise), brush the tops with the milk and bake for about 15 minutes OR until the tops are partially golden. Serve with Satsuma (see page 164), Banana (see page 165) or Strawberry Jam (see page 161), or Blood Orange and Passionfruit Curd (see page 21) and lightly whipped Crème Chantilly (see page 214).

Blueberry Pancakes & Spiced Orange Syrup OR Banana Pancakes & Spiced Lime Syrup

Early on in the year I had to confront the strange fact of never having made a decent pancake in my life – sometimes it's the simplest things that can elude you. After a month of anguish testing many recipes, finally I arrived at this delicious result.

Syrup

zest of 2 oranges OR limes
1 cup (250ml) orange juice OR 180ml lime juice
¾ cup (175g) caster sugar
1 cinnamon stick, broken in half
2 star anise

Batter

1½ cups (375ml) milk
¼ cup (60ml) white vinegar
2 eggs
2 teaspoons natural vanilla extract (+ 3 teaspoons ground cinnamon if using bananas)
3 tablespoons melted butter
2 cups (300g) plain flour, sifted
3 teaspoons baking powder, sifted
4 tablespoons caster sugar
½ teaspoon salt

1 x 4cm cube of unsalted butter
1 cup fresh or frozen blueberries OR 1 large banana, peeled and thinly sliced

Créme Fraîche Anglaise

½ cup (125ml) créme fraîche
1 teaspoon vanilla bean paste
1 tablespoon icing sugar, sifted

To make the *syrup*, combine all the syrup ingredients in a small saucepan and bring to the boil. Reduce to a simmer and stir until the sugar is dissolved. Cover, remove from the heat and set aside to infuse further.

To make the *batter*, mix the milk and vinegar in a jug. Add the eggs, vanilla and melted butter, then mix to combine. In a medium mixing bowl combine all the dry ingredients and the wet mixture, then whisk until smooth.

Heat a non-stick frypan over medium heat, stab halfway into the cube of butter with a fork and grease by whizzing it over the surface of the hot frypan. Ladle about ½ cup of batter into the frypan then drop about a dozen blueberries OR banana slices evenly over the surface. When the pancake is ready to be turned over, it should have risen about 1cm, the edges cooked and the surface pitted like a crumpet. Flip and cook on the other side until golden.

To make your *crème fraîche Anglaise*, beat the crème fraîche, vanilla and sugar – to soft or stiff peaks is up to you.

Serve hot pancakes with a drizzle of the syrup and a dollop of the crème fraîche Anglaise on top.

> If you prefer plain pancakes like me, simply omit the fruit and serve with maple syrup.

> Whenever using citrus, try to cook it as little as possible. Gentle heat is excellent for infusion and a fresh vibrant flavour will be retained. Aggressive heat will create a murky marmaladey flavour.

Hazelnut & Fresh Fruit Torte

I've been making this dessert for years and it's definitely a crowd pleaser. I usually fill the layers with a mixture of kiwi, banana, raspberries and strawberries, which gives a nice variety of colours and textures but just one type of fruit can also be terrific. This torte base is essentially a pavlova with hazelnut meal folded in at the end. Hazelnut meal is one of my besties in the kitchen – there is virtually no dessert that can't be made better by substituting at least some of the flour content in a recipe with hazelnut meal.

Torte Base

6 large egg whites, at room temperature
1⅓ cups (300g) caster sugar
1½ cups (165g) hazelnut meal
1 teaspoon red wine vinegar

2 cups (500ml) cream
⅓ cup (40g) icing sugar
1 teaspoon vanilla bean paste OR
   natural vanilla extract

Filling

the fruit needs to be sliced before the
   ganache is made
3 bananas, sliced into 5mm thick pieces
2 punnets strawberries, sliced into
   5mm thick pieces
3 kiwifruit, peeled, halved, sliced into
   5mm thick pieces

Ganache

100ml cream
100g dark chocolate, chopped

Special Equipment: electric cake mixer

Preheat the oven to 140°C or 130°C fan-forced. Line 3 baking trays with baking paper and draw a 20cm diameter circle on each sheet. Set aside.

To make the *torte base*, beat the egg whites in a large clean mixing bowl (preferably stainless steel or glass) with an electric cake mixer until soft peaks form. Keep beating, gradually adding 1 tablespoon of the caster sugar at a time. Beat until all the sugar is incorporated and you have a meringue with stiff peaks. Sprinkle with the hazelnut meal and vinegar and gently fold into the meringue. Divide into 3 batches and spread evenly onto the trays using the drawn circles as a guide. Bake for 1 hour (if you are using 2 levels of your oven, swap the trays at halfway time) then switch the heat off and leave in the oven to cool completely – overnight is best. You may prep these up to a few days before and store in an airtight container.

In a medium bowl combine the cream, icing sugar and vanilla and whip until stiff peaks form. Refrigerate until required.

To make the *ganache*, heat the cream in a small saucepan over medium heat until bubbles begin to appear. Remove from the heat, add the chocolate and stir until all the chocolate is melted and the mixture is smooth. Be careful not to overboil the cream as it will separate and give you a lumpy ganache. Allow ganache to rest for 1–2 minutes then fill a small icing bag with a 2mm nozzle.

Begin to assemble the torte by placing one of the torte bases onto a plate or cake stand. Spread one-third of the cream on and then fan out different types of the sliced fruit so the colour is nicely distributed. Zig zag one-third of the ganache over the first layer of cream and fruit. Repeat the process with another layer of the torte base, cream, fruit and ganache on the second and top layer. You may chill the torte for a short while but it is best to assemble it shortly before serving.

When beating egg whites, always make sure you have a very clean dry bowl and well separated eggs as any fat content will prevent the albumen from frothing up properly.

Instead of the crème chantilly, you may use the leftover egg yolks to make a chocolate crème patissiere to fill the layers with (see page 212).

Kuih Lapis (Indonesian Layer Cake)

There are many Malaysian sweets that are made with this layered effect but this Indonesian one really 'takes the cake'. I have many childhood memories of sitting with other children and eating it the only way it should be eaten and that is by gently peeling each layer off, then gleefully dangling it into your mouth. I have been questioned several times about my use of Chinese five spice instead of mixed spice in this recipe, but this is how my mum made it all through my childhood, so consider it the right way for the Yeow family!

390g unsalted butter, softened

2 cups (250g) icing sugar

1 teaspoon vanilla extract

15 egg yolks

120g plain flour

½ teaspoon baking powder

2 teaspoons Chinese five spice

6 egg whites

2 tablespoons brandy

vegetable oil, for greasing

Special Equipment: 20cm square cake tin + electric cake mixer

Cream the butter with half the icing sugar and the vanilla extract with an electric cake mixer until pale and fluffy. Beat the yolks in one at a time, add the flour, baking powder and Chinese five spice, then mix with a whisk.

Beat the egg whites with an electric cake mixer until soft peaks form. Add remaining icing sugar, 1 tablespoon at a time, mixing until stiff peaks form and all icing sugar is used. You should be able to tip your bowl of egg whites upside down without it budging one iota! Whisk one-third of the egg whites into the cake mixture then gently whisk the remainder in. Add the brandy and whisk gently to combine.

To prepare the cake tin, brush well with vegetable oil, then line the cake tin carefully with baking paper. Spread a heaped ⅓ cup of mixture evenly on the bottom surface of the tin and grill on a moderate heat (if it can be controlled) until golden. Remove the tin from the oven and spread another ⅓ cup of mixture over the surface and return to the grill – there is no need to cool the previous layer first. Repeat until all the mixture is used. Cool in the tin completely before running a knife around the edges, turning it out and slicing into small 1 x 4cm slices. Serve with tea or coffee.

As your cake gets higher you might want to grill the cake on a lower rung in the oven to ensure the layers aren't browning before they are cooked through. Also don't be greedy for a completely even golden surface each time. If you know it's cooked, move onto the next layer or your cake will wind up very dry and tough – Kuih Lapis should be very moist and dense with a fine crumb.

Sweet Cheeses!

Marie's Baked Berry Cheesecake

For so many years I swore that a baked cheesecake just wasn't my thing – too heavy, too rich. Then one day my friend Matt came over and literally force-fed me a spoonful of the most delicious, mysteriously light, berry-filled cheesecake. It was from Marie, his neighbour, who on giving me the recipe promised that 'At least fifty Greeks will be lining up to buy your book if you publish my cheesecake recipe', which I found hilarious, so thanks, Marie, for THE best baked cheesecake recipe in the world.

Base
200g Digestive biscuits
85g unsalted butter, melted

Cream Cheese Layer
400g cream cheese
2 large eggs
100g caster sugar
1 teaspoon vanilla bean paste OR
　natural vanilla extract

Sour Cream Layer
1 teaspoon vanilla bean paste OR
　natural vanilla extract
450ml sour cream
40g caster sugar

Topping
¼ cup (55g) caster sugar
⅓ cup (80ml) water
250g frozen mixed berries
1 teaspoon arrowroot, OR wheaten
　cornflour

Special Equipment: 20–22cm non-stick springform tin + mortar and pestle + food processor

Preheat the oven to 190°C or 180°C fan-forced.

To make the *base*, crush the biscuits with a mortar and pestle OR blitz in a food processor until you achieve a sandy texture. Transfer the crumbs into a medium mixing bowl, add the butter and stir to combine. To be rid of a potentially troublesome lip, release the base from your springform tin, turn it upside down and re-clamp into place. When it's time to serve, your cake will now slide off the base with ease. Line the base with some baking paper, then press the crumb and butter mixture evenly onto it. Set aside.

Combine the *cream cheese layer* ingredients in a food processor and blitz until smooth. Pour over the biscuit base ensuring the surface is nice and smooth, then place on a baking tray to bake for 20 minutes until set. Remove from the oven and rest for 20 minutes.

Place the *sour cream layer* ingredients in a medium mixing bowl and whisk until combined. Pour over the cream cheese layer and return to the oven to bake for another 10 minutes. Cool, then chill in the refrigerator for at least 8 hours or overnight.

To make the *topping*, place the caster sugar in a small saucepan with 2 tablespoons of water over low heat and stir until the sugar has dissolved. Increase the heat to medium, add the berries, cover and simmer for 3–4 minutes OR until the berries begin to soften. Remove from the heat and allow to cool, then chill.

In a small bowl, mix the arrowroot and 2 tablespoons of water, then add to the saucepan of berries and stir until smooth. Return to a low heat and cook until the juice thickens and turns translucent. Set aside to cool.

To serve, remove the cheesecake from the tin and spoon the fruit topping over the top.

Lychee & Amaretti Cheesecake

I'm mad about this combination, inspired by ye olde Dim Sum dessert special, almond jelly with tinned lychees. I made it as a tongue-in-cheek experiment once and my dinner guests loved it!

Base

90g Digestive biscuits

70g amaretti biscuits*

75g unsalted butter, melted

Filling

1 cup lychee purée made from fresh OR tinned lychees (if tinned, drain and discard syrup)

7–8g gold-strength gelatine leaves, soaked in plenty of cold water for 10 minutes

375g cream cheese, softened

½ cup (115g) caster sugar

1 tablespoon lime juice

2 tablespoons Paraiso Lychee liqueur

1 cup (250ml) cream, whipped

Topping

1 cup lychee purée made from fresh OR tinned lychees (if tinned, drain and discard syrup)

3 teaspoons caster sugar

3 teaspoons cornflour

few drops pink or red food colouring

7 peeled and deseeded lychees, for decorating

Special Equipment: 20–22cm non-stick springform tin + mortar and pestle + electric cake mixer

To make the *base*, crush the biscuits using a mortar and pestle OR blitz in a food processor until you achieve a sandy texture. Transfer the crumbs into a medium mixing bowl, add the butter and stir to combine. To be rid of a potentially troublesome lip, release the base from your springform tin, turn it upside down and re-clamp into place. Line the base with some baking paper, then press the crumb and butter mixture evenly onto it and refrigerate. When it's time to serve, your cake will now slide off the base with ease.

To make the *filling*, heat ¼ cup of lychee purée with the gelatine leaves in a small saucepan over low–medium heat and stir until gelatine leaves dissolve. Allow to rest for 5 minutes. With an electric cake mixer, beat the cream cheese, sugar, lime juice and lychee liqueur until smooth. Add the remainder of the lychee purée and the gelatine mixture then beat until just combined. Add the cream and gently whisk by hand until just combined. Refrigerate for 2 hours OR until filling is set.

Prepare the *topping* only when the filling is set. To achieve a smoother texture for the topping, push the purée through a sieve and discard the pulp (optional). Mix the sugar and cornflour with 2 teaspoons of the lychee purée until smooth. Add to the remaining purée in a small saucepan and whisk to combine. Bring to the boil then reduce to low–medium heat and stir for about 3 minutes until the mixture thickens to the texture of custard. Add 2–3 drops of pink or red food colouring to achieve the palest of pinks, allow to cool for 5 minutes then pour over the set filling.

To make lychee frangipanis, slice lychees from the hollow centre to the bottom centre leaving a small radius of space so the petals hold together, place on topping and refrigerate for another hour. This cake is set with a minimum quantity of gelatine, which makes it incredibly soft and creamy rather than bouncy. The disadvantage of this is that it doesn't hold as well, but if this bothers you just add another 2g gold-strength sheet of gelatine to the recipe.

*Amaretti biscuits are available in the baked goods or the Italian section at supermarkets, or gourmet delis.

Chocolate

I'm sure there isn't a single person on the planet who doesn't love breaking through the lightest of cake crusts into a warm, gooey pot of chocolate. This is my faithful emergency recipe, for the times when I have dinner guests and not enough time to make dessert. It's easily and quickly executed, even with spectators watching intently!

125g unsalted butter + extra, for greasing

2 teaspoons plain flour + extra, for ramekins

125g dark chocolate, chopped

2 eggs + 2 yolks

2 tablespoons caster sugar

Special Equipment: electric cake mixer + 4–5 small ramekins

Preheat the oven to 200°C or 190°C fan-forced.

To prepare the 'pots', use a pastry brush to grease the ramekins (or heatproof teacups are a sweet alternative) with melted butter. When brushing the sides, use an upward stroke as this will help the batter rise evenly. Scoop a teaspoonful of plain flour into each ramekin, then shake it around to coat the buttered surface thoroughly. Tap each ramekin upside down on a benchtop to remove any excess flour.

To make the batter, melt the butter in a small saucepan over low heat. Turn heat off and add the chocolate. Shake the pan so the butter coats the chocolate and allow to rest for about 2 minutes. Stir to ensure chocolate is melted and emulsified with the butter. Set aside.

Combine the eggs, yolks and sugar in a medium mixing bowl and beat with an electric cake mixer until the mixture is thick and moussey. Add flour and chocolate mixture and fold together until combined, then pour immediately into prepared ramekins. You can prepare the pots up to this stage and refrigerate for a few hours, then bake when required.

Bake pots for 8 minutes for a runny centre or 9 minutes for a firmer centre, then whisk them to the dining table IMMEDIATELY as the tops will sink fast, but warn your guests of HOT pots! Serve with a jug of unwhisked Crème Chantilly (see page 214) so the cream is of a pouring consistency.

Instead of using vanilla, you could mix a dash of Grand Marnier or Frangelico into the Crème Chantilly.

Folks, this is a REAL red velvet cake made from beets instead of ridiculous amounts of red food colouring. If you're turning up your nose at what seems an unlikely marriage, try it first. The combination of earthy beets, bitter, smoky dark chocolate and slightly salty cream cheese is heavenly! Totally Unicorn is a heavy metal band and my brother-in-law, Mikey, is their illustrious drummer. Whenever they go on tour and stay with us, this is what they get for supper after a night of intense head banging.

Cake Batter

300g (about 5 medium-sized) beetroots, leaves and root tips trimmed off
3 large eggs, whisked
1 teaspoon natural vanilla extract
125g unsalted butter
100g dark chocolate (70% cocoa), roughly chopped
200g caster sugar
220g plain flour, sifted
2 teaspoons baking soda, sifted
100g dark drinking chocolate powder, sifted

Cream Cheese Icing

125g cream cheese, softened
½ cup (60g) icing sugar, sifted
50g unsalted butter, softened
1 tablespoon lemon juice

Dark Chocolate Ganache

100ml cream
100g dark chocolate (70% cocoa), roughly chopped

Special Equipment: disposable rubber gloves + round 20cm cake tin + blender OR stick blender + electric cake mixer

Preheat the oven to 180°C or 170°C fan-forced.

To make beetroot purée, wrap each beetroot in foil with 1 teaspoon of water in each parcel and place in a heatproof dish to roast for 30–45 minutes, depending on the size of the beetroot. The beets are ready when tender enough to be pierced without much resistance, much like a potato.

Remove the foil wrapping from the beets, cool for 5 minutes and then rub the skins off. Wear gloves as they will shield you from the heat and red stain of the beets. Weigh out 250g of beets, then chop roughly and pulverise with a blender OR stick blender. Cool for about 5 minutes then whisk in the eggs and vanilla until combined.

Turn oven down to 170°C or 160°C fan-forced. Line the cake tin with baking paper.

Heat the butter in a small saucepan over low–medium heat. When melted, remove from the heat and add the chocolate. Stir or whisk until chocolate is melted and the mixture is smooth, then add to beetroot mixture and whisk until combined.

In a medium mixing bowl whisk the dry ingredients briefly, then add the chocolate beetroot mixture and stir with a whisk until just combined. Pour into the prepared tin and bake for 45–50 minutes OR until an inserted skewer comes out clean. Cool for 5 minutes before turning the cake out onto a cake rack, then cool completely before icing.

To make the *cream cheese icing*, simply bung all the ingredients except the lemon juice into a medium bowl and beat with an electric cake mixer until very pale and fluffy. Add the lemon juice last and beat until just combined.

To make the *chocolate ganache*, heat the cream until bubbles begin to appear then immediately remove from the heat and whisk in the chocolate until the mixture is smooth. Be careful not to overboil the cream or it will separate and give you a lumpy ganache. Allow ganache to rest for 1–2 minutes.

continued over page...

To assemble, slice cooled cake horizontally in half. Spread the icing evenly on one half and sandwich back together. Meanwhile, tuck small lengths of baking paper (about 10 x 20cm) partially under the cake to catch any falling ganache – this will keep the edges of your plate clean. Pour the ganache over the cake and, using a spatula or butter knife, guide the ganache over the sides. Keep scooping the cascading ganache from the bottom of the cake and spreading it upwards until it stops running, then leave it alone or it will lose its gloss from overworking. To finish, use your spatula to create a soft, swirly pattern, then remove the baking paper carefully and the cake is ready to serve.

If you are concerned about losing your spot after slicing the cake in half, simply make a vertical notch on the side of the cake. After icing, lining up the 2 parts of the notch, which will help you to place the top and bottom layers where they originally were, giving you a nice flat cake to ganache and any dodgy slicing will be concealed!

Flourless

Flourless Hazelnut & Chocolate Fudge Cookies

Makes 15–20 cookies

This is my go-to recipe when I have very little time and some leftover egg whites. The cookies have an intense cocoa flavour and a wonderful chewy texture similar to that of a brownie. If you are a chocolate fiend the batter will easily tolerate the addition of chopped chocolate or chocolate chips. As for the method, you could practically do it with your eyes closed!

105g OR 3 extra large egg whites

1½ cups (190g) icing sugar

¼ teaspoon salt

1 cup Dutch process cocoa or high-quality baking cocoa

1 teaspoon instant espresso coffee powder (optional)

zest of 1 orange (optional but with pistachios this is a particularly good pairing)

1½ cups (180g) roasted hazelnuts OR pistachios, very roughly chopped

1 cup chopped chocolate OR chocolate chips (optional – if using, reduce quantity of nuts to 1 cup. It's up to you the ratio of each but the mixture will tolerate 2 cups of additions.)

Special Equipment: electric cake mixer OR whisk + 1–2 baking trays

Preheat the oven to 170°C or 160°C fan-forced.

Mix all the ingredients, except the nuts and chopped chocolate, with an electric cake mixer or whisk until just smooth. Add the nuts and chocolate and stir to combine. Line 2 baking trays with baking paper and dollop tablespoons of the batter onto the trays, leaving 3cm gaps between the cookies. Bake for 8 minutes. When the cookies are out of the oven the surface should be slightly cracked and glossy like a brownie. Cool on a wire rack completely before storing in an airtight container in the fridge. These are best eaten within 2 weeks.

Gluten-Free Jaffa Almond Cake

Being a hugely enthusiastic baker, the words 'gluten-free' used to send me into a tailspin. Several years ago, I acquired a mystery illness that suggested I might be gluten intolerant and I was nothing short of mortified. Luckily this wasn't the case, but I've since learnt that there is no need to be so fatalistic. There are now a great number of products available in healthfood shops and supermarkets which yield brilliant results and ensure gluten-intolerant food lovers out there aren't missing out. This recipe is based on the classic Jewish Passover orange & almond cake, but I've added chocolate because it's a match made in heaven. Gluten-intolerant or not, you'll find this recipe dee-lish – not too sweet and beautifully moist with an intense choc-orange flavour.

2 very good quality oranges with firm
    skins, unpeeled
8 large free-range eggs
1⅓ cups (300g) caster sugar
100g unsalted butter
200g dark chocolate (70% cocoa),
    broken or roughly chopped into
    small pieces
2 tablespoons Dutch process cocoa or
    high-quality baking cocoa
1 teaspoon vanilla bean paste OR
    natural vanilla extract
3 cups (300g) almond meal
150g gluten-free plain flour
1 teaspoon gluten-free baking powder
icing sugar, for dusting

Special Equipment: blender OR stick blender + electric cake mixer + 22cm round cake tin

Wash the oranges and place in a medium saucepan then cover with water and bring to the boil. Turn the heat down and simmer for 2 hours with the lid ajar. Keep a close eye on the water level as it can evaporate very quickly. Have a kettle of boiled water nearby to top up the water if necessary.

Drain the oranges and allow to cool. Slice the oranges into quarters, remove the seeds and purée skin and all using a blender OR stick blender. Up to this point the recipe can be prepared up to 2 days ahead of time.

Preheat the oven to 180°C or 170°C fan-forced and line the cake tin with baking paper. Place the eggs and caster sugar in a medium mixing bowl and beat with an electric cake mixer until pale, fluffy and tripled in volume.

Melt the butter in a small saucepan over medium heat. Remove from the heat, add the chocolate, then jiggle the saucepan around so the hot butter coats the chocolate. Cover and wait for about 1 minute, then stir the mixture until emulsified and smooth. Cool for a minute or two.

Add the orange purée and the remaining ingredients except icing sugar to the egg and sugar mixture and mix gently with a whisk until combined. Add the butter and chocolate mixture, continuing to mix gently with a whisk until combined. Pour the batter into the prepared tin and bake for 1 hour OR until an inserted skewer comes out clean. Cool and dust with icing sugar to serve. An elegant option is to cover the cake with Dark Chocolate Ganache (see page 218).

Pandan & Palm Sugar

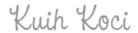

Kuih Koci

Makes 8 dumplings

Kuih Koci is my favourite kuih. It's a lovely shredded coconut mixture cooked in coconut cream and dark palm sugar stuffed into a delightfully chewy dough made from glutinous rice flour. The sweet dumpling is then wrapped in fresh banana leaves, shaped into a pyramid and steamed. If you are already feeling insecure about the folding part, you can simply pop your stuffed kuih with the seam facing down on a square of banana leaf, then steam.

Stuffing

½ cup (125ml) coconut cream

70g gula melaka* (dark palm sugar), sliced

15g caster sugar

¼ teaspoon salt

1 pandan leaf*, shredded lengthways by hand and tied in a knot

1 cup (60g) dried shredded coconut

2 tablespoons boiling water

Dough

230g glutinous rice flour*

100–150ml coconut milk

70g sweet potato steamed and mashed finely

1 tablespoon vegetable oil

2 teaspoons sugar

generous pinch of salt

¼ teaspoon pandan paste* (pandan aroma pasta)

banana leaves, stalks removed, cut into 12 x 20cm squares

vegetable oil, for greasing

Special Equipment: vegetable steamer with 10cm high sides

To make the *stuffing*, combine the coconut cream, sugars, salt and pandan leaf in a small saucepan and bring to the boil. Reduce to a simmer and stir until the sugars are dissolved, then turn heat off. Mix the coconut with the boiling water in a small mixing bowl until all the water is absorbed, then add to the sugar and coconut milk mixture in the pan and return to a medium heat. Stir continuously and cook until there is no runny liquid left but the mixture is still very moist. Set aside to cool.

To prepare the banana leaves, blanch in boiling water for 1–2 minutes making sure all leaves are submerged. Plunge into iced water to retain colour (if you care enough!). Dry each leaf individually with a clean tea towel, then with a pastry brush grease both sides generously with vegetable oil. Set aside.

To make the *dough*, mix all the dough ingredients in a medium mixing bowl and knead until smooth. Roll the dough into a fat cylinder and divide into 8 even-sized balls. Cover the dough with cling wrap and work with one piece at a time. Coat your hands in vegetable oil then, using your thumb, gently press into the ball while continuously rotating it to create a well in the centre and until the dough is about 5mm thick all around. Stuff a teaspoonful of filling into each ball and gather the sides to seal. Dip the balls into vegetable oil, rolling them around in your hands to distribute the oil evenly over the entire surface and rest on an oiled plate or tray.

To fold the banana leaves, hold the parallel sides of a leaf then bring them together while using your fingers to guide the centre of the square to form a cone. Place a ball into the cone and press gently, then fold the sides over the dumpling as you would when gift wrapping the sides of a parcel, to form a square base. If any of the banana leaves tear you will need to use a new leaf. Place the wrapped parcels in a steamer and steam, covered, over rapid boiling water for 10 minutes. Serve at room temperature.

Kuih should be eaten on the day it is made. It's not ideal to store it in the fridge but if you do, you'll need to revive the hardened dough by re-steaming it over rapid boiling water for 7–10 minutes.

*Available from Asian grocers

Pandan Sago Pudding with Coconut & Dark Palm Sugar

This is possibly the simplest Malaysian dessert you can make. It's always a talking point at parties because people who have never tried it before find the texture and appearance of the tiny sago pearls fascinating. The delicious trilogy of pandan, coconut and gula melaka (dark palm sugar) is a recurring combination in many South East Asian desserts.

4 L water

1 cup (195g) sago*

½ egg white whisked to soft peaks (optional but helps pearls separate when eating)

½ teaspoon pandan paste* (pandan aroma pasta)

vegetable oil, for greasing

¾ cup (150g) gula melaka* (dark palm sugar), sliced

2–3 tablespoons water

1⅔ cups (410ml) coconut milk (if very thick, water down 1 cup (250ml) coconut milk to ⅔ cup (160ml) cow's milk)

¼ teaspoon salt

Special Equipment: 5 x 250ml dariole moulds or jelly moulds, OR 1 L bunt tin

Boil the water in a medium pot, and rain in the sago, stirring immediately to separate the grains, and cook until the pearls are translucent. If there is a small dot of white at the centre of the pearls, don't be concerned. Drain the sago in a sieve, then rinse thoroughly with cold water until all excess starch is washed away and the pearls feel cool to touch. Transfer to a medium mixing bowl and fold in the beaten egg white and pandan paste until just combined. Lightly grease moulds and fill with the sago, then cover with cling wrap and refrigerate for a minimum of 30 minutes for individual serves and 1 hour for the bunt tin. Overnight refrigeration is also fine.

Melt the palm sugar with the water in a small saucepan over low–medium heat. Set aside to cool to room temperature then chill in the fridge.

In a small saucepan bring the coconut milk and salt to the boil, then allow to cool and chill in the fridge.

To serve, turn out the puddings from the moulds and if you have used a bunt tin, slice into wedges. Pour ⅓ cup of coconut milk and 1 tablespoon of palm sugar over each serve. To eat, use a spoon to press down and break the pearls apart, then mix all the components together.

*Available from Asian grocers. Sago is available from supermarkets or Asian grocers and is sometimes labelled tapioca pearls.

Tantalising Tarts

Chocolate Hazelnut Paté Sablée with Blood Orange & Passionfruit Curd

There's nothing I hate more than waste and this little number literally came about from me bunging two sweet leftovers together. If you want to fancy it up, the Lavender Chantilly provides a lovely perfumed note against the sharp citrus flavours and earthy, rich sablée.

leftover Paté Sablée from Rhubarb
   Lily Tart (see opposite page)

1 portion of Blood Orange &
   Passionfruit Curd (see page 21)

Lavender Chantilly (optional)
1 cup (250ml) cream
½ tsp dried lavender buds
2 tablespoons icing sugar
1 teaspoon vanilla

Special Equipment: 12 x 6.5cm round tart tins with removable bottoms OR muffin tins + 9–10cm round pastry cutter

To make the *lavender Chantilly*, heat the cream in a small saucepan over low heat until just warm. Add the lavender, cover and remove from the heat to cool. Refrigerate overnight, then strain through a sieve to remove the lavender. Add sugar and vanilla and whisk until medium–stiff peaks form and set aside.

Preheat the oven to 180°C or 170°C fan-forced.

Use a pastry cutter to cut circles of pastry and place them into the tart tins, making sure the inside corners are pressed in. It's much easier to use a blob of pastry to do this rather than your fingers, pressing it into the sides. If you are using a muffin tin, only press the pastry halfway up the sides, otherwise they will require too much filling. It doesn't matter if the edges are a bit wonky and rustic – it will look quite charming. Bake for 10–15 minutes and immediately press down to remove any bumpy surfaces while the pastry is still hot and malleable. Fill with Blood Orange and Passionfruit Curd or freeze cooked pastry shells for a rainy-day dessert.

Serve tarts with a small dollop of lavender Chantilly on the side.

Rhubarb Lily Tart

Of all the recipes in this book, this is probably the one I'm most proud of because it literally came to me in a dream inspired by a failed challenge I had on *MasterChef* when I attempted to cook rhubarb and make the pieces stand upright. I painted water lilies obsessively as a young artist, so it was lovely that the solution came to me in this form. I literally bounced out of bed, bought the ingredients, chopped, moulded and baked like a fiend and a few hours later, the Rhubarb Lily Tart was realised.

Rhubarb

6 broad pieces of orange peel, making
    sure to avoid any pith
10–12 thick stalks of rhubarb, at least
    2–3 of which are thinnish, cut into
    4cm pieces
1 vanilla bean, split, seeds scraped out,
    pod reserved
⅓ cup (80g) caster sugar

Hazelnut Cocoa Paté Sablée

180g raw caster sugar
1 cup (110g) hazelnut meal
260g plain flour
½ cup (60g) Dutch process cocoa OR
    good-quality baking cocoa
2 pinches of salt
200g unsalted butter, room temperature,
    diced into 2cm cubes
1 egg, whisked

Orange Crème Anglaise

6 egg yolks
70g caster sugar
200ml milk
200ml cream
1 vanilla bean, split, seeds scraped out
    and pod reserved OR 1 teaspoon
    vanilla bean paste
zest of 1 orange

Special Equipment: 2 x 7–8cm ramekins + pastry cutters

Preheat the oven to 100°C or 90°C fan-forced.

Line the base of each ramekin with 3 pieces of orange peel. Cut one end of each piece of rhubarb into an arrowhead. In a small bowl, rub the vanilla seeds and caster sugar together, then toss the rhubarb pieces in and coat thoroughly. Tightly pack the rhubarb into the ramekins working from the outer edge into the centre, with the thinner pieces in the centre and the arrowheads pointing up. Cover with foil and bake for 2 hours – the slow cooking on very low heat produces the most silken, flavourful threads. Remove from the oven and allow to cool to room temperature.

To make the *sablée*, combine all the dry ingredients in a medium–large mixing bowl, then break the cubes of butter into the flour mixture and rub vigorously with your hands until you have a sandy consistency. Add the egg and rather than knead, use a gathering, squeezing action to bind the mixture into a ball. Turn and knead a few times to smooth dough out, then roughly shape into 2 discs. Cover each disc with cling wrap and rest in the fridge for 30 minutes.

Preheat the oven to 180°C or 170°C fan-forced. Roll the dough out to a 3–4mm thick piece and with a pastry cutter, cut 2 x 10cm circles, 2 x 8cm circles and 2 x 6cm circles for the 6 lily pads. With the back of a knife, score lines across each lily pad, dividing it into 12 pie shapes to represent the veins of the leaf. Rest the lily pads in the freezer for 10–15 minutes before placing on a baking tray lined with baking paper and bake for 10–15 minutes. If the lily pads emerge from the oven with a few bubbles, immediately press them down with a spatula while the pastry is hot and malleable.

To make the *crème Anglaise*, whisk the yolks with the caster sugar in a medium mixing bowl until pale and moussey. Combine the milk, cream, vanilla seeds and pod, and orange zest in a medium saucepan. Bring to the boil, remove vanilla pod, then pour into the yolk mixture. Whisk briefly before returning the mixture to the saucepan and stir over low heat until it thickens to the consistency of pouring cream. Do not boil. To test if custard is ready, dip a wooden spoon in and draw a line across the centre of the back of the spoon with your finger. When the custard is ready, the line will stay put. If drips immediately form, cook it a little longer. If the custard has split, quickly transfer to another bowl and blitz with a stick blender as this might salvage the texture.

continued over page...

To assemble the rhubarb lily tart, cup your hand over the ramekin. Carefully tip the cooked rhubarb upside down into the palm of your hand over a bowl to catch the syrup. Place a slotted egg flip over the flat rhubarb ends and flip it over quickly so the arrowheads face up. Balance the egg flip with rhubarb over a bowl and drain the residual syrup. Arrange the lily pads on a large plate, slide the rhubarb onto the plate and gently push the pieces of rhubarb down to make the lily flowers. If you have an attractive single serve jug, fill with the orange crème Anglaise and place on the plate.

Very little of the Paté Sablée is used for the Rhubarb Lily Tart but making a small amount doesn't make sense. I always cut and press the remainder of the pastry into little tart tins and bake them to fill with whatever is in season. A couple of good options are the Blood Orange and Passionfruit Curd (see page 21) or strawberries with Crème Chantilly (see page 214) and a drizzle of balsamic.

Bibs
& Bobs

Achar Penang (Spicy Vegetable Relish)

This is a very popular Malaysian pickle or relish. Typical of Malaysian dishes, its flavour base comes from a rempah, an intense aromatic paste with a good amount of heat. Traditionally achar is eaten as a snack, with rice or in this case as a side dish for Nasi Lemak.

Vegetables

¼ cabbage

2 continental cucumbers, quartered
   lengthways, seeds sliced off

2 large carrots

250g white Chinese radish

200g snake or stringless beans

4 L water

¼ cup (60ml) vinegar

3 teaspoons table salt

Rempah – Pickling Sauce

8 cloves garlic, peeled and sliced

12 red eschallots OR 2 medium Spanish
   onions, peeled and roughly sliced

15 small + 5 large dried red chillies*
   seeds removed, snipped into small
   pieces, covered in freshly boiled water
   for about 30 minutes or until soft

3cm galangal*, peeled and finely sliced

4cm turmeric root*, peeled and finely
   sliced OR 3 tsp ground turmeric

2 stalks lemongrass*, pale part only, dry
   outer layers removed, finely sliced

180ml (¾ cup) vegetable oil

1 cup (250ml) water

⅔ tablespoon brown sugar

1–2 teaspoons salt OR to taste

3–4 tablespoons white vinegar OR
   to taste

300g roasted, salted crushed peanuts

Special Equipment: good-quality blender OR mini food processor OR mortar & pestle

Slice all the *vegetables* into 5mm thick, 4cm long batons. In a large saucepan, bring the water, vinegar and salt to the boil. Add the vegetables and blanch for 5 seconds. Drain and leave to cool in a colander (overnight in the fridge is best). After cooling, transfer the vegetables to a colander lined with a clean tea towel or muslin and squeeze out as much of the liquid as possible. Set aside.

To make the *rempah*, combine the garlic, red eschallots, chilli and chilli water, galangal, turmeric and lemongrass in a blender and blitz to a fine paste. Heat the oil in a heavy bottom non-stick saucepan or wok over medium heat and cook the rempah, stirring continuously until most of the moisture has evaporated and the paste is fragrant and caramelised. Add the water, sugar and only 1 teaspoon of salt for the time being. Bring to the boil, add the vinegar and peanuts, then reduce the heat to a simmer and cook for about 30 seconds or until the sauce is thick. Season further if required then cool for 15 minutes before mixing with the vegetables in a large mixing bowl and transferring into clean, sterilised glass jars** to refrigerate. Achar is best eaten after 3–4 days of pickling and will last for up to 1 month in the fridge.

*Available from Asian grocers and some supermarkets and greengrocers. For notes on dried chillies, see page 226.
**For notes on sterilising, see page 219.

Chocolate Crème Patissiere

Pipe into choux pastry, slather between layers of cake or use as a cream base for tarts.

6 egg yolks

90g caster sugar

pinch of salt

To make crème patissiere, combine the yolks, caster sugar, salt, cornflour and cocoa in a medium mixing bowl and whisk until pale and thick. In a medium heavy-based saucepan, bring the milk and cream to the boil, then pour over yolk mixture

2 tablespoons wheaten cornflour

2 tablespoons Dutch process cocoa

1 cup (250ml) cream

1 cup (250ml) milk

100g dark chocolate, chopped
(70% cocoa)

and whisk to combine. Return the custard mixture to the saucepan and cook over medium heat, stirring continuously for 5 minutes, until the custard thickens. Add the chocolate and stir until melted. Cover with clingwrap directly on the surface of the custard to prevent a skin forming and allow to cool. Chill completely before using.

Chocolate Ganache

. . . .

This is a very versatile method for adding some glamorous gloss and flavour to any cake. This amount will easily cover a round cake 20–22cm in diameter and up to 7cm high.

100ml cream

100g dark, milk or white chocolate,
chopped

Heat the cream in a small saucepan over medium heat until small bubbles begin rising to the surface. Remove from the heat, add the chocolate and jiggle the pan to coat chocolate with the hot cream. Cover and allow to sit for 1 minute, then stir with a silicone spatula or metal spoon until smooth. Allow the ganache to cool for 2 minutes before pouring and spreading over the cooled cake with a spatula. This will make it less runny and more manageable. If the ganache is still rather fluid and pooling at the bottom of the cake simply use your spatula to scoop the excess ganache and sweep it back over the sides. When it stops cascading, do not be tempted to go over the surface again. Overworking the ganache when it begins to set will take away the gloss and you will be left with a dull, matt finish (still yum though!).

To avoid making a mess of the ganache, sit your cake on desired serving dish then tuck strips of 6 x 20cm baking paper all around the underside of the cake. This will shield your platter from any falling ganache. To finish, gently pull the strips of paper away to reveal a nice clean edge without the daunting task of transferring the cake onto a clean platter!

Crème Anglaise/Ice-Cream

Makes about 800ml

. . . .

Crème Anglaise is a basic pouring custard and becomes the base for any ice-cream when churned in an ice-cream churner. You may add melted chocolate, any fruit purée, infuse with liqueurs or zest of citrus.

200ml cream

200ml milk

4–5 large egg yolks*

70g caster sugar

1 teaspoon vanilla bean paste, natural
vanilla extract, OR 1 vanilla bean,
seeds scraped out and pod reserved

200ml fruit purée of choice if making
ice-cream

*More yolks will create a thicker, richer custard but sometimes I feel it tastes a little too eggy

Special Equipment: electric cake mixer + ice-cream machine

In a medium saucepan bring the cream and milk to the boil with reserved vanilla pod (if using) then set the saucepan aside. Meanwhile whisk the yolks, sugar and vanilla until pale and fluffy. There's a lot of fuss that surrounds this next bit, which usually tells you to pour slowly and whisk madly at the same time. But the yolks are already stabilised or 'blanched' by the sugar so you can just plonk it all together in one fell swoop then whisk. Return the combined mixture to the used saucepan and cook over low heat, stirring continuously, until it thickens slightly. It should not at any point bubble or boil as high heat will split the custard.

To test whether the custard is just right, dip a wooden spoon into the mixture then run a finger across the back of the spoon. If the custard is cooked the line you've drawn with your finger will stay put. If not, drips will immediately form. Keep cooking and conducting the wooden spoon test every minute. If you split the custard, immediately transfer it to a mixing bowl and whisk with an electric cake mixer on high speed as this might salvage the texture. If it's beyond help, don't sweat – it'll still taste delicious if a little lumpy. Serve warm, chilled or churn in an ice-cream machine following the manufacturer's instructions. For a cheaper churner, make sure the custard and fruit purée (if using) is completely chilled – overnight is best.

A little cheat's secret for avoiding splitting the anglaise is to add 1 teaspoon of wheaten cornflour when whisking the yolk, sugar and vanilla mixture. This will stabilise and thicken the mixture a little.

Clarified Butter

Makes about 180g

Clarified butter is butter that's been heated gently to separate the water content and milk solids from the butter fat. When the butter fat has been rendered out, it has a much higher smoking point so it won't burn with the use of high heat like regular butter. It also has a longer shelf life than regular butter when unrefrigerated.

250g good quality unsalted butter, diced

Heat the butter in a heavy-based saucepan over low heat. Wait for butter to melt and allow to simmer very gently. The butter will splutter a little at this stage and a foamy surface will emerge. Skim this off with a small sieve or ladle until the spluttering dies down and no more foam seems to be rising. Line a sieve with muslin or cheesecloth and strain the liquid into a heatproof bowl or jug. Pour into a sterilised glass jar* and store unrefrigerated for up to 3 months or in the fridge for up to 12 months. The yield will be about ¾ of its original amount.

*See page 219 for notes on sterilising glass jars

Crème Chantilly

Makes about 300ml or 1¼ cups

Crème Chantilly is really just a fancy name for a sweetened cream with a bit of vanilla in it. It's very useful for taking the edge off sweet desserts and of course provides a bit of luscious moisture.

300ml cream
2 tablespoons icing OR caster sugar
1 teaspoon vanilla bean paste OR
    natural vanilla extract

Special Equipment: electric mixer OR stick blender

Combine cream, sugar and vanilla in a mixing bowl. You can whip the cream using a stick blender with the aerating attachment, an electric cake mixer or a good old-fashioned whisk. Beat to soft peaks for a pillowy mouthfeel or take it to stiff peaks for more structure and slathering between layers of cake.

Crème Fraîche

Crème fraîche is a brilliantly versatile ingredient that you can easily make at home. Use it in place of regular cream in a Chantilly and it immediately adds character to conventional desserts – the hint of sharpness carried by the live culture is great for cutting through sweet things. Crème fraîche is also excellent for savoury dishes because it doesn't split over high heat like conventional cream.

2 cups (500ml) milk
3 tablespoons buttermilk

Heat the milk in a small saucepan over very low heat until lukewarm to touch – any hotter and the heat will kill the culture. Stir in the buttermilk and transfer the mixture to a clean, sterilised glass jar*. Fasten the lid and leave it in a warmish spot at room temperature for 24 hours. You will find the mixture has thickened slightly. Remove the lid, stir and leave in the fridge for another 24 hours and it will be ready to use. This will keep in the fridge for up to 2 weeks.

*See page 219 for notes on sterilising glass jars

Gnocchi

I've come full circle with gnocchi. I used to swear by kipflers, and their high starch content almost guarantees your gnocchi won't fall apart at boiling stage, but I've also used just about every type of common and less expensive potato with excellent results – make sure you don't overcook and waterlog the potatoes and you'll be fine.

1kg potatoes, skins scrubbed and
    left on
200g plain 00 flour
1 egg, lightly whisked
100g Parmegiano Reggiano or best
    Parmesan you can afford, finely
    grated
salt
chopped parsley, to serve

Special Equipment: mouli OR potato ricer

To make the gnocchi, place the potatoes in a large pot with plenty of water and bring to the boil. Boil until potatoes are tender and the tip of a knife is easily inserted. Drain and cool briefly. Hold potatoes with a teatowel or oven mitt in one hand and peel with the other. To mash potatoes, mill with a mouli OR press through a potato ricer OR mash with a fork and push through a sieve. Place the mashed potato, flour, egg and Parmesan in a large bowl. Gather ingredients in a circular motion and then squeeze (rather than knead) the mixture gently until it binds into a large ball. The texture should feel like very soft playdough but it shouldn't stick to your hands. Dust the bench with a small amount of flour, break small sections of dough away and roll gently into 1cm wide tubes. With a knife, cut 1.5cm sections, roll them in plenty of plain flour and rest them on a tray ready to boil.

In a large pot, boil plenty of water (1 tablespoon salt to 1 L water). Shake excess flour off gnocchi before tossing into the boiling water. When gnocchi pieces are cooked they will float. Wait a few seconds before scooping them out with a slotted spoon and lowering gnocchi straight into sauce – this avoids double handling. Don't stir but gently scoop gnocchi out with sauce and portion into bowls. Serve garnished with grated Parmesan and a sprinkle of chopped parsley.

Neutral Chicken Stock

I call this a neutral chicken stock because no herbs or aromatics are involved, which allows for some versatility depending on what style of food you are cooking.

2kg chicken carcasses
4–5 L water

Special Equipment: large stock pot

Combine the chicken carcasses and water in a large stock pot. Bring to the boil uncovered and then reduce the heat, cover and simmer over very low heat for 2–3 hours, skimming the frothy impurities off the top as you go along. Remove bones, strain stock through a fine sieve or muslin, cool and refrigerate so all the fat solidifies and is easily removed and discarded. Divide into portions and freeze.

If you want a more precise flavour (or rather, if you could be bothered), infuse afterwards by simmering over the lowest heat, covered, for 15–30 minutes with bashed ginger and a few knotted stalks of spring onion for Asian-style dishes and for European dishes, use a bouquet garni: 1 bay leaf, 4 sprigs thyme, 1 sprig rosemary, 6 sprigs fresh flat-leaf parsley, 2 sprigs celery leaves if you have some, tied into a bundle with kitchen string.

The Perfect Hard-Boiled Egg

Use few-day-old eggs because fresh eggs don't peel well.

In a saucepan, cover any amount of eggs with an excess of 2–4cm of water but make sure there is only one layer of eggs. Bring to the boil, then immediately cover and remove from the heat. Rest for 11–12 minutes depending on how hard you want the centres, then peel and use as desired.

Perfect Rice by absorption method

There are so many methods that people swear by when it comes to cooking rice. I've always been frustrated by the old-fashioned Chinese first knuckle method that I was raised with. In my twenties a Korean workmate taught me the Mt Fuji way. As you can imagine both methods are so variable and nothing irks me more than dishing up mushy rice. Measuring the water and precise timing consistently produces a perfect, fluffy result.

1½ cups (375ml) water to every 1 cup (200g) of rice – traditionally we wash the rice 3 times, then drain

Special Equipment: large stock pot

As an option you may toast the rice with a fat of some sort at the beginning like ghee, butter or coconut oil and add a teaspoon of salt for extra seasoning.

If you are cooking a large amount of rice, I would recommend splitting the rice into 2 pots or cooking it in a bigger saucepan. The large surface area means the heat won't have to travel too far up. Also the grains on the bottom won't get compressed and mushy while the top might be slightly undercooked.

Make sure the rice is well drained (for about 10–15 minutes) in a sieve. Combine it with the water in a pot that will accommodate the rice doubling its original volume. Bring rice to the boil, then cover and simmer for 10 minutes until no water is visible and the surface of the rice is pitted with holes. Reduce to the lowest heat possible and cook for another 10 minutes, then turn heat off and keep covered for another 5–10 minutes before loosening grains with a fork or chopsticks. Keep covered until required.

Pulut Santan (Steamed Glutinous Coconut Rice)

2 cups (400g) glutinous rice*, soaked overnight in plenty of water

1⅓ cup (330ml) coconut milk

1 teaspoon salt

¼ teaspoon pandan paste (optional)*

Special Equipment: large pot & lid + 5cm high trivet + 20cm round cake tin

To make pulut santan, drain the rice in a sieve for 15 minutes before transferring to a medium mixing bowl and combining with the coconut milk, salt and pandan paste. Stir, then pour into a 20cm cake tin lined with foil. Place tin on a 5cm high trivet in a large deep pot and fill with enough water to reach the bottom of the tin. Cover and steam over high heat for 30–40 minutes OR until the rice is tender to the bite. Have a kettle with freshly boiled water nearby so you can top up the water as regularly as you need it – I have been caught out smoking instead of steaming my glutinous rice many times! Cool completely in the tin before attempting to lift the slab of cooked rice out and cutting into 3 x 3 x 1cm squares. Serve with a generous dollop of kaya (see page 20) on top.

*Available from Asian grocers

Rough Puff Pastry

Makes about 700g

1⅔ cups (250g) plain flour

1 teaspoon salt

250g unsalted butter, sliced 1cm, slightly softened*, the butter should be easily broken by hand but still firmish

120ml chilled water

To make the rough puff, combine the flour and salt in a medium mixing bowl and mix roughly. Break chunks of butter into the flour and rub briefly, leaving most of the chunks intact, then add 90ml of the water. Using a squeezing action, gather the mixture so it is barely sticking together. It's a good sign if some parts are quite crumbly. If it seems very dry, add the remainder of the water. Shape the dough into a squarish slab, cover with cling wrap and rest for 20 minutes in the fridge.

Dust a clean benchtop lightly with flour and roll the pastry in one direction into a rectangle 3 times longer than it is wide (roughly 39 x 13cm). The pastry should look a bit of a crumbly mess and marbled at the beginning but it will sort itself out as you roll it out. Fold into thirds and give it a quarter turn so the layered seams are facing you. Repeat this rolling process another 3 times, then rest in the fridge for 30 minutes before using.

> The trick to a successful rough puff is to handle your pastry minimally and work quickly. If at any point during the 'laminating' process you find your pastry is getting very limp, immediately refrigerate for 20 minutes. It is important that you don't let the butter get too soft or it will be absorbed more easily by the dough and after all your hard work, the layers won't separate well.
>
> Watch out for the desired marbled effect – if it's not noticeable, you might have over-handled the dough and inadvertently made shortcrust pastry via the scenic route – been there, done that! It's still perfectly good to use, you'll just have a different but equally delicious outcome.

Sambal Belachan

Sambal Belachan is a much loved condiment of Malaysian households. It's very useful to have around because you can create a huge amount of instant flavour by adding it to noodle, soup or rice dishes. There are many types using slight variations of a similar recipe but Sambal Nasi Lemak is my favourite. I love to mix it into a mountain of rice with a couple of fried eggs and freshly sliced cucumber to cool the lips.

Sambal Nasi Lemak

20g belachan*

20 small + 5 large dried red chillies*, deseeded, snipped into small pieces, covered in freshly boiled water for about 30 minutes OR until soft

5 long red chillies, sliced

3 teaspoons tamarind paste*

½ cup (125ml) vegetable oil

3 medium brown onions, peeled and sliced

3 tablespoons caster sugar OR to taste

salt to taste

Preheat the oven to 180°C or 170°C fan-forced.

To prepare the belachan, wrap in a double layer of foil and roast for 15–20 minutes OR until dry, crumbly and fragrant. Blitz in a food processor with the rehydrated dried chillies and chilli water, and fresh chillies and tamarind paste until a fine paste forms.

Heat the oil in a medium saucepan over medium heat. Add the chilli paste, stirring and cooking until the mixture is a thick deep amber. When the sambal is adequately caramelised, the oil will begin to pool around the edges of the saucepan and separate from the mixture. Add onions and sugar and season carefully as the belachan is high in salt. As soon as the mixture begins to bubble again, remove from the heat. If the paste is very thick, add a few tablespoons of water to loosen the mixture. Taste at the very end to see if more sugar, salt or tamarind is required for balance. Store in an airtight container in the fridge for 1 month or 3 months in the freezer.

*Available from Asian grocers. For notes on dried chillies see page 226.

Sambal for Tearaway Dumpling Soup

20g belachan*

20 small + 10 large dried red chillies*, deseeded, snipped into small pieces, covered in freshly boiled water for about 30 minutes OR until soft

6 red eschallots, peeled and quartered

½ cup (125ml) vegetable oil

2 tablespoons caster sugar OR to taste

salt to taste

To prepare the belachan, wrap in a double layer of foil and roast for 15–20 minutes OR until dry, crumbly and fragrant. Blitz in a food processor with the chillies and chilli water and red eschallots until a fine paste forms. Heat the oil in a wok or frypan over medium heat, add chilli paste and cook until the mixture is thick and a deep amber. When the sambal is adequately caramelised, the oil will begin to pool around the edges of the wok or frypan and separate from the mixture. Add the sugar, then season carefully as the belachan is high in salt. Taste at the very end to see if more sugar or salt is required for balance. Stored in an airtight container, this will keep in the fridge for up to 1 month or in the freezer for 3–4 months.

*Available from Asian grocers. For notes on dried chillies see page 226.

Tamarind Paste from scratch

Makes about ⅓ cup

1 golfball-sized chunk of tamarind, torn from a dried brick of tamarind pulp*

½ cup (125ml) hot water

*Available from Asian grocers

To make tamarind paste from scratch, steep the tamarind in half a cup of hot water for about 10 minutes and massage the pulp with your hands until homogenised. Press the mixture through a sieve. Scrape the resulting paste from the bottom of the sieve, then use as desired. Discard pulp. The leftover paste may be frozen in an ice cube tray for later use.

Quatre Épices (French Four Spice)

Quatre Épices is a spice blend that is very versatile and used commonly in Europe in charcuterie, sauces and gravies. If you make it yourself you will find many variants on the ratios and even recipes that break the four in the four spice but this is the one from my good friend Emmanuel Mollois.

1 tablespoon whole white peppercorns

2 teaspoons freshly grated nutmeg

2 teaspoons whole cloves

1 teaspoon ground ginger

Special Equipment: spice mill OR mortar & pestle

Grind all the spices to a fine powder using a spice mill OR mortar and pestle. I don't like using electric spice grinders as much because they use a cutting rather than grinding action so you get very uneven grains. Store in an airtight container in a cool, dark spot in the pantry.

How to Sterilise Glass Jars

To sterilise glass jars, submerge jars in a large pot of boiling water for a few seconds. Transfer to a tray lined with 2 layers of newspaper and place in oven on 120°C or 110°C fan-forced for 20 minutes. Turn oven off and only take jars out as you need them, so they don't cool down. A quicker way is to microwave for 30 seconds after submerging in the boiling water. Just a word of warning, don't fill the jars with cold food, or the dramatic change in temperature will cause the glass to break – hot food into hot jars is the rule.

Conversion Chart

1 teaspoon = 5ml
1 Australian tablespoon = 20ml (4 teaspoons)
1 UK tablespoon = 15ml (3 teaspoons/ ½ fl oz)
1 cup = 250ml (8 fl oz)

Cup Measures

1 cup almond meal	100g	3½ oz
1 cup sugar, brown	185g	6½ oz
1 cup sugar, white	220g	7¾ oz
1 cup caster (superfine) sugar	230g	8 oz
1 cup (confectioner's) sugar	125g	4⅓ oz
1 cup plain (all-purpose) flour	150g	5½ oz
1 cup long grain uncooked white rice	200g	7¼ oz

Liquid Conversions

cups	metric	imperial
⅛ cup	30ml	1 fl oz
¼ cup	60ml	2 fl oz
⅓ cup	80ml	2 ½ fl oz
½ cup	125ml	4 fl oz
¾ cup	180ml	6 fl oz
1 cup	250ml	8 fl oz
1½ cup	375ml	12 fl oz
2 cups	500ml	16 fl oz
4 cups	1 L	32 fl oz

Glossary

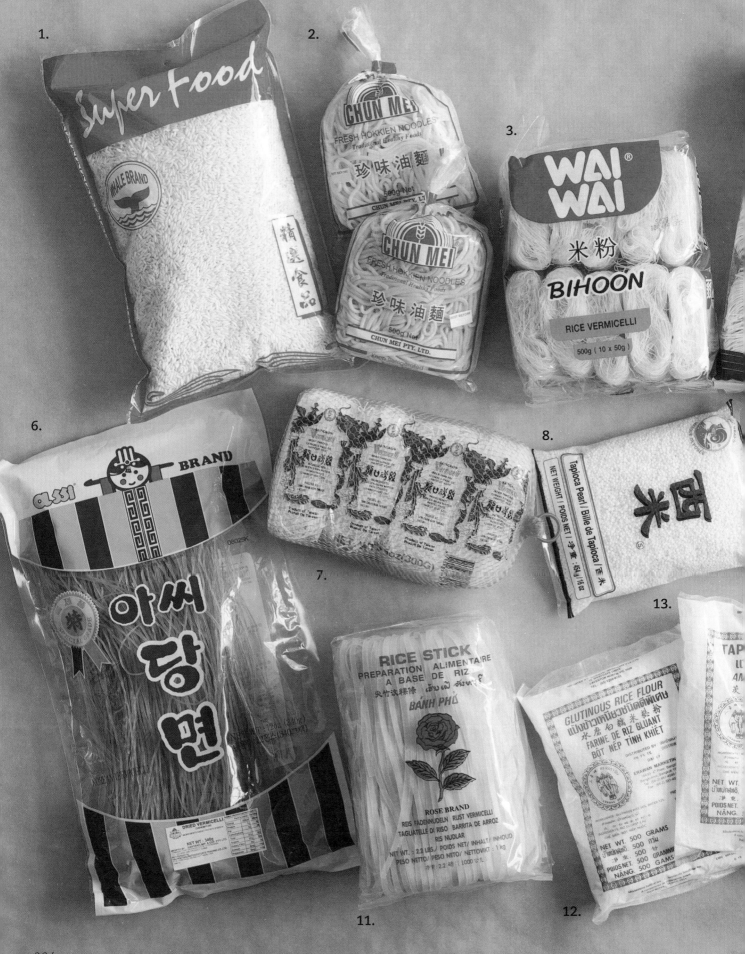

1.

2.

3.

6.

7.

8.

13.

11.

12.

224

To help you shop...

All available at Asian grocers, *found in some supermarkets. On the next few pages I've picked a selection of products to help you identify the right ingredients and packaging. There is a wide range of brands available.

1. Glutinous Rice
Must be soaked before using. Contains no gluten, high in starch, chewy, bouncy texture, used in desserts and savoury foods throughout Asia.

2. Hokkien (Egg) Noodles*
Difference between the pale and yellow type is food colouring! Used in stir-fries, soups.

3. Thin Rice Noodles* (Bihoon/Mai Fun/Rice Vermicelli)
Used in stir-fries and soups.

4. Dried Chinese Egg Noodles*
Mild flavour, good for stir-fries and soups.

5. Rice Paper*
Avoid frying as they tend to burst. Best eaten fresh after dipped into hot water and stuffed immediately. Also don't dunk for too long or the rice paper gets soggy and tears easily.

6. Korean Sweet Potato Starch Noodles
Quite flavourless, thick translucent threads with a springy texture. Great for stir-fries, salads and soups.

7. Glass Vermicelli (Dried Cellophane Noodles)
Quite flavourless, clear threads usually made from mung bean starch, interesting springy texture. Good in stir-fries, soups and stuffings.

8. Sago (Tapioca Pearls)*
Quite flavourless, clear, jelly-like beads. Processed from the central pith of a sago palm and different from tapioca pearls which are made from the tapioca tuber. However, packaging often will be labelled as both being the same thing. Just look for white, 2mm beads and you'll be sorted.

9. Konnyaku (Shirataki) Noodles
Rich in fibre, low calories, low carbohydrate. Translucent jelly-like noodles with a crunchy texture. Flavourless, good for soups.

10. Rice Sticks/Noodles*
Thicker than bihoon, otherwise same. Good for stir-fries, soups, stuffings.

11. Dried Vietnamese Flat Rice Stick Noodles*
These can be used instead of fresh versions which come in the fridge section. Lovely slippery texture, good in stir-fries and soups.

12. Glutinous Rice Flour
Contains no gluten, ground glutinous rice flour. When kneaded with water or coconut milk and steamed or boiled, produces a chewy, sticky texture. Used in Asian desserts and savoury dumpling skins.

13. Tapioca Starch
Used in Asian desserts, dumpling skins, noodles. Produces a springy, chewy texture, otherwise quite flavourless.

14. Potato Starch
Used mainly in dumpling skins and noodles.

15. Wheat Starch*
Same as commercially produced wheaten cornflour. Mostly used as a thickening agent. Used in dumpling skins and noodles.

Meat Curry Powder
Also fish and vegetable blends. Not your average curry powder even though that has its place!

Pickled Mustard (Haam Choy) Salty, crunchy, mildly earthy flavour. Very versatile – good for stewing, stir-fries, steaming.

Dried Anchovy (Ikan Bilis) Salty, very yummy fried, can be added to chicken stock for added flavour and seasoning.

Black Moss (Faat Choy)
Yes, it looks like a bad-quality toupee! Musky, mushroom flavour, slippery texture when cooked.

Century Egg (Preserved Egg)
Very sulphurous in odour and flavour, whites are a translucent black and have a jelly-like texture, yolks can be slightly runny, usually with grey-greenish hued rings. Definitely an acquired flavour, often eaten with rice congee.

Azuki (Red) Beans Mostly used in Asian sweets. Taste similar to a lot of pulses, most often boiled, mashed and cooked with sugar to form a paste then stuffed into things like buns, mochi, glutinous rice flour dough and pancakes.

Dried Shrimp
Many types. Salty, intense shrimp flavour. Some South East Asians use it dry but it's usually soaked first. Many applications – used in stir fries, steamed savoury cakes, salads, soups.

Korean Chilli Powder (Aka Gochugaru)
For making kimchi.

Dried Red Chillies* Several types available. Use a combination of small and large ones to adjust the spiciness to your liking – smaller ones are the hottest and the broader, larger ones, mild. If you are using all small chillies because you love the heat, still throw in at least 5 large ones to boost colour and chilli flavour. You can replace dried chillies with fresh ones, but you won't get the slightly smoky rounded heat and depth of colour of the dry ones.

Sechuan Peppercorns
Beautifully fragrant, peppery and numbing on the mouth.

Tamarind Paste*, Tamarind Pulp, Tamarind Slices Fruity flavoured, souring agent for curries, marinades, salad dressings, stir-fries.

Cloud Ear (Black Fungus) Needs to be soaked before using. Relatively tasteless, used mainly for texture. Used in stir-fries, soups, dumplings.

Wakame One of many types of dried Japanese seaweed. Salty, flavour of the sea, umami, mainly used in soups.

Dried Tigerlily Buds (Gum Chum) Doesn't sound as exotic but technically these are day lily buds, slightly crunchy, mild, grassy mushroom flavour. Not a common ingredient, but can be used in stir-fries, soups, steamed dishes.

Dried Shiitake Mushrooms Need to be soaked before using, robust flavour, meaty texture, used widely across Asia in everything. Good for stir-fries, braising, steaming, soups, stuffings.

Dried Bean Curd Sticks (Foo Jook) Flavour of soya beans, slippery texture if braised. Used mainly in stews, soups.

Shredded Cuttlefish or Squid Rehydrate before using, pungent fishy flavour, chewy texture, good for everything – stir-fries, steaming, soups, dumplings.

1. Pandan Paste (Pandan Aroma Pasta) The more convenient option to fresh pandan leaves. Avoid essence versions as they are usually not good. Very pungent grassy, jasmine scent. Used widely throughout South East Asia in sweets like vanilla is used in the West.

2. Wasabi* Japanese condiment mostly used to accompany sushi.

3. Coconut Milk/Cream* Ask your Asian grocer which brands to buy as there are very few that provide an authentic flavour and many bad imitators.

4. Belachan* Malaysian-style, fermented shrimp paste. Very pungent, fishy flavour which dissipates on cooking. Usually roasted before used in aromatic pastes, chilli pastes.

5. Salted Plums

6. Tinned Pickled Cabbage Good for stir-fries and soups.

7. Dark Palm Sugar (Gula Melaka) Malaysian- or Indonesian-style palm sugar. Look for the cylinders that you can dent with your nail through the packaging and for a dark brown. If the colour is translucent amber and the sugar very hard, avoid it as it won't be the real stuff but caramelised sugar. Unlike Thai pale palm sugar, this is used only in sweets. Usually paired with coconut and pandan.

8. Fermented Chilli Bean Curd Salty yeasty flavour, breaks into a paste. Good in stir-fries, braises and soups.

9. Tinned Straw Mushrooms

10. Fermented Brown Beans Excellent for steaming, stir-fries and soups.

Fridge & Freezer

All available at Asian grocers, *found in some supermarkets.

1. Spring Roll Pastry or Wrappers*
Usually fried but these can be stuffed and steamed instead.

2. Fish Cakes
Good for noodle soups, noodle and rice stir-fries. Handy to have in the freezer.

3. Soft Tofu* (Soy Bean Curd)
Good for soups, hot pots and steaming. Mild nutty flavour.

4. Fried Tofu Puffs (Soy Bean Curd)
Used in soups and braises. Can be stuffed with salad and eaten cold or stuffed with meat and then steamed or boiled.

5. Fish Tofu
This is technically not a tofu but the name alludes to the soft slightly bouncy texture. The only soy in it is soy oil. Very handy to have in the freezer. Good for stir-fries and soups.

6. Frozen Soy Beans (Edamame)
Excellent for stir-fries or used in place of frozen peas.

7. Firm Tofu* (Soy Bean Curd)
Very versatile, good for stir-fries, stews and soups.

8. Flying Fish Roe (Tobiko)
Most commonly found on sushi but also good as a garnish on canapés and salads. Salty, sweet, provides good pop-in-your-mouth sensation.

Shaoxing
(Shao Hsing)
Rice Wine

Korean
Fish Sauce

Fish
Sauce*

Oyster
Sauce*

Chilli Oil

Seasoning

All available at Asian grocers, *found in some supermarkets

Light Soy
Sauce*

Dark Soy
Sauce*

Caramel
(Thick) Soy
Sauce

Kecap Manis*

Chinkiang
Vinegar

231

Yam Bean (Jicama)
Similar to water chestnut.
Crunchy, refreshing, watery
with mild earthy flavour.
Excellent for stir-fries.

**Chinese White
Radish (Daikon)**
Watery, crunchy root
vegetable. Used in
many Asian cuisines
for pickles, soups and
stir-fries.

Celeriac* Root
vegetable. Flavour and
texture is cross between
celery, potato and turnip.
Excellent in place of
mashed potato to have
with any fish or meat.

Taro Root or tuber, not
to be confused with yam.
Commonly used ingredient
in Hakka cuisine. Usually
steamed first, then fried,
stir-fried or mashed
and cooked with other
ingredients. Good with
duck especially as a crust.
Earthy flavour, very starchy.

Choy Sum*
Chinese green,
good for stir-
fries and soups.

Pak Choy*
Chinese green, good
for stir-fries and soups.

Bok Choy*
Chinese green, good
for stir-fries and soups.

Fennel Bulb*
Can be braised but
best freshly sliced in
salads. Crunchy with
aniseed flavour.

Fresh

All available at Asian
grocers, *found in some
supermarkets

Spring Onions* Also called long green onions, scallions and shallots. Good for stir-fries, salads and as a garnish.

Red Eschallots* Also called shallots. Sweeter and more aromatic than regular onions when cooked.

Ginger* Spicy, throat warming, earthy rhizome. Much loved aromatic across all of Asia. Used in sweets and savoury cooking.

Turmeric* Rhizome related to ginger. Earthy, bitter sweet, stains a rich, vibrant yellow. Used widely in Indian, South East Asian and Middle Eastern cuisines.

Pandan Leaf is not eaten but used to infuse most South East Asian desserts and sometimes used in savoury cooking. Flavour is an intense jasmine. Commonly used to add perfume to rice and usually paired with palm sugar and coconut in desserts. Fresh and frozen are both good to use.

Galangal* Rhizome also related to ginger but with a stronger citrus perfume. Tough hard skins and woody flesh unless very young. Used mainly in South East Asian cuisine.

Curry Leaves* (Sweet Neem Leaves) Highly aromatic leaf, used mostly in India and surrounding countries.

Enoki Mushrooms The texture of the thin crunchy stem is almost valued more than the cap. Subtle flavour, faintly musky and used for stir-fries, soups, salads and sometimes deep fried.

Chrysanthemum Greens Asian green from an edible chrysanthemum species. Good in soups and stir-fries.

Lemongrass Wonderful citrus flavour, very fibrous and needs to be chopped finely or pulverised. Can be bashed and infused into soups, great in stir-fries and fish cakes. Remove dry outer layers and only use the white part.

233

Equipment

I'm not sure about you but when I started cooking, not knowing my kitchen equipment resulted in a few culinary misadventures, so I'll quickly outline the job each one does.

Bamboo Steamer
Good for steaming anything that will fit, but limited by height and quite annoying to wash, so make sure you line it with baking paper every time, then poke lots of holes in the paper to let the steam pass through OR rest each item on a small square of baking paper.

Stick Blender
Great for puréeing directly in a vessel, for instance when you are making soup in a pot and, with the aerating attachment, it is also suitable for whipping cream and making foams if you are a fancy pants cook.

Mortar and Pestle
Very useful for making pastes, like rempahs, pestos, chilli and guacamole, but it's also great for crushing dry ingredients like nuts or biscuits. Beware of strong flavours from your aromatics getting embedded in the granite and transferring onto ingredients for sweet dishes. A 20cm diameter Asian-made granite one is the most useful size and texture. Anything much bigger can get difficult to handle, and the ingredients tend to creep up the sides rather than staying in the middle where you are pounding. I'd avoid anything with a smooth texture as they don't achieve much except that they are easier to clean.

Mouli
A hand-cranked device used for milling soft fruit or cooked vegetables into a purée. It's often used for potatoes to make gnocchi.

Electric Cake Mixer
Hand held or with a stand. You would be mad not to own at least one of these because creaming butter until it's pale and fluffy or beating eggs by hand involves a lot of elbow grease! The whisk attachment is used for aerating, the paddle for mixing a stiffer batter like cookie dough and the dough hook is of course for kneading dough. Do make sure you have it on the slowest setting for this job or you'll burn out the engine very quickly. I owned a hand-held mixer for ten years. This is an essential for baking and you can pick up very cheap ones that last for ages.

Pastry Cutters
A set of these is a versatile thing to have in the kitchen. Apart from the obvious, you can also use them for creating height and structure when plating things that might otherwise scatter on a plate (a bit nouvelle '90s though!) or even for pressing burger patties if you want a uniform shape.

Whisk
An indispensable tool to have in the kitchen, not just for aerating ingredients but a great mixing tool, especially for removing lumps from batters and breaking up mince meat.

Chinese Spider
Comes in various sizes and particularly useful for deep-frying. Enables you to easily collect many cooked items in one fell swoop, which is important when frying as things can turn from golden to incinerated within seconds!

Blender
NOT what you make pastry with – a lesson I learnt 15 years ago as a novice cook! A blender is really only good for puréeing soft, already broken down food like cooked veggies or meat, and raw fruit. A decent amount of liquid is required in the mixture for the blades to move effectively, but it WILL crush ice very well.

Mini Food Processor
Excellent for chopping small quantities of ingredients and is able to break down fibrous matter like galangal, lemongrass and dried chillies better than a larger food processor.

Food Processor
Chops differently from a blender. It is capable of finely chopping (not puréeing) ingredients that don't have a high water content, like meat and nuts, very evenly, but it can be problematic when you are dealing with small quantities as the ingredients tend to get blasted to places where the blade doesn't reach, and it's not able to achieve an even or fine chop. It is, however, a good option for making pastry quickly if you are an impatient cook with hot hands.

Pasta Maker
I had never owned one of these until early this year and really, I stole it from Mum because she never uses it. This machine is brilliant – pasta, fresh Chinese noodles, I even use it to make my Mantou (Chinese Flower Buns) on page 17.

Trivets
Several of these of varying heights are very handy because they suspend any vessel over boiling water and allow the steam to circulate and provide a gentle, even heat source over the cooking food.

Potato Ricer
Looks like a giant garlic press and is used instead of mashing. I use it for cooked potatoes, taro, peas, carrots, pumpkin and bananas – essentially anything soft and starchy will pass through it.

Acknowledgments

Thank you to my beautiful, talented Joffy for being a constant anchor – eternally patient and loving; to the short tiger, Rhino, for making me laugh every minute, every day; to my culinary pillars, Mum and Koo Poh, for always allowing me midnight access to the magic pantry and for being wells of knowledge; to Dad for daring me to dream and for your die-hard, over-enthusiastic support; Casper, Teena, Trent, Tyler, Trin and Hayley for your patience and support despite my perpetual absence; Matt, for constantly reminding me that 30 more Christmases is all we can hope for (hot damn!) and egging me on to aspire for more impossible dreams; Sarah for your quiet but stoic support and creative influence in my life; to the Bennett clan, for all your love and support from afar; to all my friends and family, mammoth thanks and apologies in one for your understanding despite my habit of going awol; to my family at the ABC, I really miss you guys!

Thanks to ABC Books/HarperCollins for your enthusiasm and support for an unconventional idea, special thanks to Helen Littleton for believing in my concept and tolerating several wig outs, to Katherine Hassett for being completely unflappable and supportive through this crazy process, to Randy and Suzi for all your hard work and allowing my love of gingham to be unfettered.

Last but not least, my most heartfelt thanks to the Australian public for your unfailing support over the past four years and giving me an incredible sense of belonging.

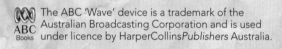 The ABC 'Wave' device is a trademark of the
Australian Broadcasting Corporation and is used
under licence by HarperCollins*Publishers* Australia.

First published in Australia in 2014
by HarperCollins*Publishers* Australia Pty Limited
ABN 36 009 913 517
harpercollins.com.au

HarperCollins*Publishers*
Level 13, 201 Elizabeth Street, Sydney, NSW 2000, Australia
Unit D1, 63 Apollo Drive, Rosedale, Auckland 0632, New Zealand
A 53, Sector 57, Noida, UP, India
77–85 Fulham Palace Road, London W6 8JB, United Kingdom
2 Bloor Street East, 20th floor, Toronto, Ontario M4W 1A8, Canada
10 East 53rd Street, New York NY 10022, USA

National Library of Australia Cataloguing-in-Publication data:
Ling Yeow, Poh.
Same same but different / Poh Ling Yeow.
9780733328312 (pbk.)
Cookery–Australia.
Australian Broadcasting Corporation.
641.5994

Art Direction, Prop & Food Styling: Poh Ling Yeow
Prop Stylist: Suzi Ting
Photography: Randy Larcombe Photography
Home Economist: Sarah Rich
Many, many thanks to the following people and suppliers who kindly let me borrow your
beautiful things – crockery, fabrics, utensils. The book would not have been possible without
your generosity and goodwill. Dandi Homewares, Fireflies, Market Import, Oxfam, little
luv, trovare, three card trick, Prints Charming, Council of Objects, Susan Frost Ceramics,
Stephanie James-Manttan Ceramics, Treehorn Design
Cover design by Matthew Phipps
Internal design by HarperCollins Design Studio
Typesetting by Alicia Freile, Tango Media
Colour reproduction by Graphic Print Group, Adelaide
Printed and bound in China by RR Donnelley on 140gsm woodfree

**Looking for more recipes from Poh: The *Poh's Kitchen* series DVDs and book are
available at ABC Shops, ABC Centres and ABC Shop online.**